hands-on
problem solving
A Minds-On Approach

Grade 1

Hands-on problem solving : a minds-on approach. Grade 1 /
Lawson, Jennifer E. (Jennifer Elizabeth), 1959-
2012   33124108059790

Senior Author
Jennifer Lawson

Writer
Pat Steuart

Project Consultant
Dianne Soltess

Mathematics Consultants
Meagan Mutchmor, Manitoba
Tina Jagdeo, Ontario
Lara Jensen, Ontario

PORTAGE & MAIN PRESS
Winnipeg • Manitoba • Canada

© 2012 Jennifer Lawson

Pages of this publication designated as reproducible with the following icon ⬚ may be reproduced under licence from Access Copyright. All other pages may only be reproduced with the express written permission of Portage & Main Press, or as permitted by law.

All rights are otherwise reserved and no part of this publication may be reproduced, stored in a retrieval system, or transmitted in any form or by any means, electronic, mechanic, photocopying, scanning, recording or otherwise, except as specifically authorized.

Portage & Main Press gratefully acknowledges the financial support of the Province of Manitoba through the Department of Culture, Heritage, Tourism & Sport and the Manitoba Book Publishing Tax Credit, and the Government of Canada through the Canada Book Fund (CBF), for our publishing activities.

Hands-On Problem Solving, Grade 1
A Minds-On Approach
ISBN 978-1-55379-338-0
Printed and bound in Canada by Prolific Group

Editor:
Leslie Malkin

Book and Cover Design:
Relish New Brand Experience Inc.

Cover Photo Credits:
@iStockphoto.com

Illustrations:
Jess Dixon

PORTAGE & MAIN PRESS

100-318 McDermot Avenue
Winnipeg, MB, Canada R3A 0A2
Tel: 204-987-3500 • Toll free: 1-800-667-9673
Toll-free fax: 1-866-734-8477
Email: books@portageandmainpress.com
www.hands-on.ca

MIX
Paper from responsible sources
FSC® C006215

Contents

Introduction to Hands-On Problem Solving Grade 1 — 1

Program Introduction — 2
Program Principles — 2
Big Ideas in Mathematics — 2
  Communication — 2
  Connections — 3
  Mental Math — 3
  Estimation — 3
  Reasoning — 4
  Technology — 4
  Visualization — 4
Problem Solving — 5
  What Is Problem Solving? — 5
  Best Practices in Teaching Problem Solving — 5
  Routine Problems — 5
  Non-Routine Problems — 6
  Extended Explorations Problems — 7
Implementing the Hands-On Problem-Solving Program — 7
  Program Format — 7
  Planning Your Year of Problem Solving — 7
  Curricular Connections — 8
  Supporting Literacy During Problem Solving — 8
  The Questioning Process — 8
  Additional Resources — 8
  A Note About Pennies — 9
Blackline Masters to Guide and Support Learning – Problem Solving — 10
Mathematics Correlation — 11
  Grade 1 Correlation Chart — 11

The Hands-On Problem Solving Assessment Plan — 13

Assessment for Learning — 13
Assessment as Learning — 13
Assessment of Learning — 14
Performance Assessment — 14
Portfolios — 14
Assessment Blackline Masters — 16

Routine Problems — 25

Implementation of Routine Problems — 26
Problem Types — 26
Teaching Routine Problems — 27
  1A Cole Finds Seashells — 32
  2A Jake Has Goldfish — 35
  3A Mrs. Kahn's Students Take the Bus — 37
  4A Charlie Makes Pattern Trains — 39
  5A Cheyenne Recycles Juice Boxes — 41
  6A Lester Has Jellybeans — 43
  7A Jan and Bob See Birds — 45
  8A Ben Sees Frogs — 47
  9A Tammy Sees Squirrels — 49
  10A Max Has a Birthday Cake With Candles — 51
  11A Cookies in a Cookie Jar — 53
  12A Bees Go in the Hive — 56
  13A Hiding Books Under the Rug — 59
  14A Jeffrey Writes a Math Poem — 62
  15A Juan Counts Boots and Shoes — 64
  16A Pam Sees Ladybugs — 67
  17A Liam Plants Seeds — 70
  18A Jacob Paints Pictures to Hang — 72
  19A Pat Is Making Pumpkin Cookies — 74
  20A Tariq and the Horses — 76
  21A Janet's Birthday Party — 78
  22A Mrs. Joyal's Class Goes Swimming — 80
  23A Hot Chocolate for the School Patrols — 83
  24A People on the Bus — 85
  25A Janey Plants Corn, Beans, and Squash — 88
  26A Ricardo Puts Money Into his Piggy Bank — 90
  27A Gobin Sees Bugs in the Garden — 92
  28A A Seesaw at Brownlee School — 94
  29A Emma Takes Gymnastics Lessons — 96
  30A Ming Makes a Pattern With Lights — 98
  31A Tina Is Making a Bracelet — 100
  32A Jeremy Makes a Pattern — 102
  33A Barry and Devon Help Build Patios — 104
  34A Max Draws Monkeys — 109

35A	Carson Measures Objects on a Scale	111
36A	Manuel Sorts Shapes	113
37A	Sherry Plays With Pattern Blocks	115
38A	Steven Makes Patterns With Shape Stickers	117
39A	Aiden Sorts Three-Dimensional Objects	119
40A	Earl Collects Tins of Soup	121

Non-Routine Problems — 123

Implementation of Non-Routine Problems		124
Teaching Non-Routine Problems		127
An Additional Resource for Solving Non-Routine Problems		129
Blackline Master to Guide and Support Learning – Non-Routine Problems		130
1B	Saving Money for the Pet Shelter	131
2B	Comparing Sunny and Rainy Days	133
3B	Trading Stickers	135
4B	Game Bags for Number Cubes	137
5B	Picking Apples for Pies	139
6B	Hat and Mitten Combinations	141
7B	Making Aliens	143
8B	Counting Robins and Spiders	146
9B	Playing on a Number Line	148
10B	Petals on Flowers	150
11B	Painting the Fence	152
12B	A Pattern for Days of School	154
13B	Making a Keychain With Beads	156
14B	Toads Eating Flies	158
15B	Clarence the Clown's Magic Bag	160
16B	A Pattern With Blocks	162
17B	Cam Chooses a Pet	165
18B	Lining Up	167
19B	Carl's Coloured Cow Counters	169
20B	Spring Party Snacks	171
21B	Rows of Shape Cookies	173
22B	Animals in the Barn	175
23B	Making a Paper Chain	177
24B	A Pattern With Shapes	179
25B	Canada Day Cupcakes	181
26B	Decorating With Flags	183
27B	Pizza Day Snacks	185
28B	Making Repeating Patterns	187
29B	Wrapping Presents	189
30B	Going for a Bike Ride	191
31B	Lindsey Plays a Board Game	193
32B	Building Model Homes	195
33B	Juan Makes New Friends	197
34B	Tables for Students	199
35B	Phillip's Toy Cars	201
36B	Monkeys on the Jungle Bus	203
37B	Coloured Bears on Numerals	205
38B	Four Rabbits Race to a Carrot	207
39B	Shannon Builds a Clay-Cube Corral	209
40B	How Many Children Are on the Play Structure?	211

Extended Exploration Problems — 213

Implementation of Extended Exploration Problems		214
Teaching Extended Exploration Problems		214
Blackline Masters to Guide and Support Learning – Extended Explorations		218
1C	Sorting Bingo Chips	219
2C	Heads or Tails?	222
3C	Making Mother's Day Bracelets	225
4C	Combinations of Blue and Yellow Cubes	227
5C	Grouping Cookies in Equal Sets	229
6C	Plants for Mr. Green's Flower Pots	232
7C	Rolling Number Cubes	234
8C	Using a Non-Standard Measurement	236
9C	Be a Shapes Detective!	238
10C	Making Numbers	241

Appendix — 243

References — 249

About the Authors — 250

Introduction to Hands-On Problem Solving Grade 1

Introduction to Hands-On Problem Solving Grade 1

Program Introduction

Hands-On Problem Solving focuses on developing students' knowledge, skills, attitudes, and strategic thinking related to mathematics through active inquiry, problem solving, and decision making. Throughout all activities presented in the book, students are encouraged to explore, investigate, and ask questions in order to heighten their own curiosity about and understanding of the world of mathematics.

Program Principles

1. Effective problem-solving programs involve students actively building new knowledge from experience and prior knowledge.

2. Development of students' understanding of concepts, flexibility in thinking, reasoning, and problem-solving skills/strategies form the foundation of the problem-solving program.

3. From a young age, children are interested in mathematical ideas. This interest must be maintained, fostered, and enhanced through active learning.

4. Problem-solving activities must be worthwhile and relate to real-life experiences. Problems should be rooted in context so that students can make sense of the numbers with which they are being asked to work in a meaningful way.

5. The teacher's role in the problem-solving process is to actively engage students in tasks and experiences designed to deepen and connect their knowledge. Children learn best by doing, rather than by just listening. The teacher, therefore, should focus on creating opportunities for students to interact in order to propose mathematical ideas and conjectures, to evaluate their own thinking and that of others, and to develop mathematical problem-solving skills.

6. Problem solving should be taught in correlation with the mathematics program and with other school subjects. Themes and topics of study in problem solving should integrate ideas and skills from the various strands of the mathematics program, as well as from other areas of study, whenever possible.

7. The problem-solving program should encompass and draw on a range of educational resources including literature and technology as well as people and places in the local community.

8. Assessment of student learning in problem solving should be designed to focus on performance and understanding and should be conducted through meaningful and varied assessment techniques carried on throughout the sections of study.

Big Ideas in Mathematics

In order to achieve the goals of mathematics education and to support lifelong learning in mathematics, students must be provided with opportunities to encounter and practise critical mathematical processes. Problem solving is one of these processes, but since they are all inter-related, it is important to recognize the characteristics of each mathematical process, and the related learning experiences for students. These processes are as follows:

Communication

Students need opportunities to share their mathematical ideas and thinking through oral language, reading and writing, diagrams, charts, tables, and illustrations. Communicating mathematically, aloud or on paper, helps students clarify their thinking for themselves and others.

▶

For example:

There are 12 goldfish.

The goldfish are in fishbowls.

Each bowl has the same number of goldfish in it.

Show different ways the goldfish could be put into fishbowls.

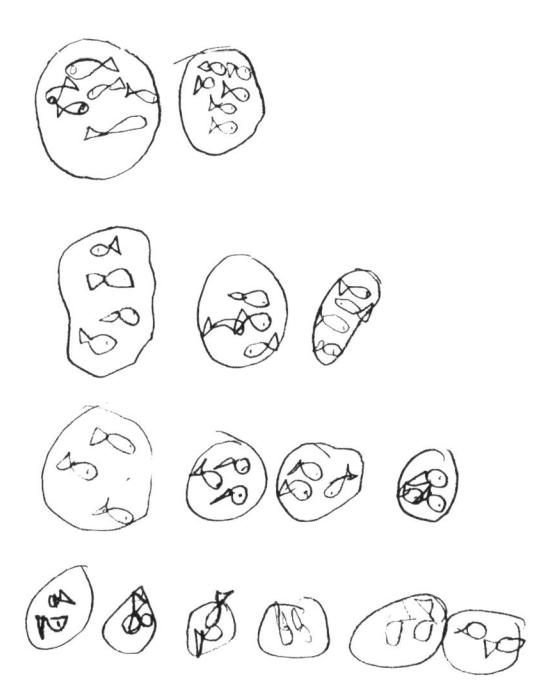

The process of communication is essential to the learning process during problem-solving investigations. Students should be encouraged to share their ideas, listen to others, and write about their problem-solving experiences, strategies, and solutions. In addition, students should be encouraged to write their own problems.

Connections

When doing problem-solving activities in the classroom, teachers should ensure that links are made between the various strands of the mathematics curriculum. It is also important to make connections between concrete, pictorial, and symbolic representations, so students should be encouraged to explore the use of manipulatives, illustrations, and symbols to solve problems. Further, concepts and skills should be connected to everyday life and to other curricular areas.

The **Hands-On Problem-Solving** program offers suggestions for connecting problem solving to other subject areas and occasionally to children's literature. Although the problem-solving activity can be successfully conducted without the literature, teachers are encouraged to acquire the occasional book suggestions and read them with students in order to correlate the problem-solving lesson with language arts and thereby enrich students' learning experience.

Mental Math

Mental math is more than just knowing the facts—it is about strategic thinking and number sense. Mental math is a process necessary to many everyday experiences, and students need extensive exposure to activities that encourage them to solve problems mentally. Strong mental math skills enable students to respond quickly to questions or required tasks phrased in a variety of ways. For example:

- Double 4
- Half of 6
- Two 5s
- You roll double 3. What's your score?
- How many shoes in 2 pairs?

Estimation

Students should be encouraged regularly to estimate quantities and measurements. Being able to make an educated guess allows students to independently check the validity of their calculations. It is also an essential skill in everyday life. Estimation encourages students to take risks, use background knowledge, and learn from the process.

For example:

Estimate whether there are enough dog houses for the dogs.

Now, check. Are there too many or too few dog houses?

Reasoning

Mathematical reasoning involves informal thinking, conjecturing, and validating. Students should be encouraged to justify their solutions, thinking processes, and hypotheses. Good reasoning is as important as finding correct answers, so students need many opportunities to think about, describe orally, and record their mathematical activities and ideas.

For example:

I am a 2-digit number.

My tens digit is 2 greater than 3.

My ones digit is 3 less than my tens digit.

What number am I?

Technology

The use of calculators is recommended, to facilitate and enhance problem-solving skills and to encourage discovery of number patterns. However, calculators must not replace development of students' number concepts and skills. Other technologies such as interactive whiteboards, computer software, and websites can provide valuable resources for students and teachers as well.

Visualization

This is the process of creating mental images needed to develop concepts and understand procedures. Visualizations help students clarify their understanding of mathematical ideas. For example:

- Show all you know about the number 17. Use pictures, diagrams, and words in your answer.

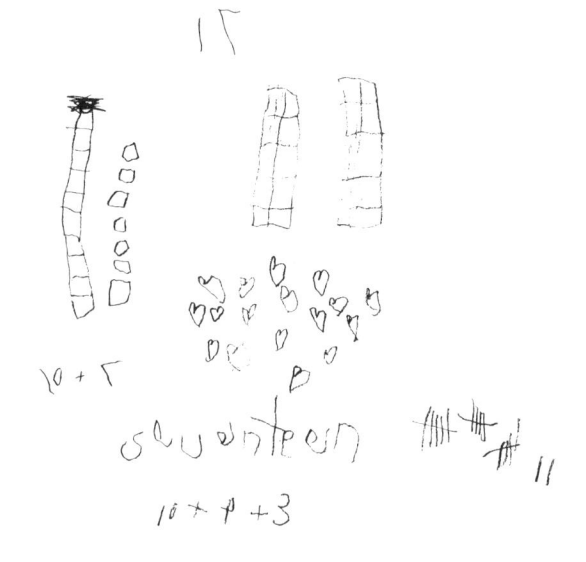

▶

4   Hands-On Problem Solving • Grade 1

Problem Solving

Problem solving is another of the "big ideas" in mathematics—the mathematical processes students need in order to achieve the goals of mathematics education and to support lifelong learning in mathematics. Students are exposed to a wide variety of problems in all areas of mathematics in **Hands-On Problem Solving**. They explore a variety of methods for solving and confirming their solutions to different types of problems. They should also be encouraged to find multiple solutions for problems and to create their own problems.

What Is Problem Solving?

Problem solving refers to "mathematical tasks that have the potential to provide intellectual challenges for enhancing students' mathematical understanding and development" (Cai and Lester, NCTM). Problem solving is the application of mathematical knowledge, tools, and strategies to a wide range of math problems in order to solve them.

Problem solving:

- Is a life skill
- Creates a purpose for learning skills and concepts
- Motivates students by developing a sense of inquiry
- Allows students to demonstrate their understanding of mathematical concepts and skills in meaningful contexts
- Teaches perseverance.

Problem solving should be the main focus of mathematics instruction. The ability to apply their knowledge to solve problems is the goal for all students.

Best Practices in Teaching Problem Solving

Problem solving is often not viewed positively by students. In order to change this perception teachers should

- Use a problem-solving approach when introducing and teaching concepts and skills;
- Begin with simple problems so students can experience success;
- Include a balance of routine, non-routine, and extended exploration problems;
- Encourage the use of multiple strategies for solving problems;
- Provide opportunities for students to write their own problems;
- Use modelling (think aloud) to demonstrate the thinking processes involved in solving a problem. Students will be reluctant to attempt a problem if they do not know where or how to begin;
- Provide time for reflection (journaling, summarizing, and so on) in order to clarify mathematical ideas and relationships;
- Encourage discussion (turn-and-talk, whole class, and so on) to develop and reinforce critical and creative thinking skills.

Routine Problems

These are problems in which the way to a solution is generally straightforward. The solution usually involves one or two arithmetic operations.

Problem Types

Efforts are made to offer a variety of types of routine problems for students to solve in **Hands-On Problem Solving**. As such, those problems focusing on number concepts include the following operations and problem types:

- Addition and subtraction: beginning unknown, middle unknown, and end result unknown

- Multiplication: product unknown
- Division: quotitive and partitive division.

These problem types are described in detail in the Implementation of Routine Problems section (see page 26).

Non-Routine Problems

These problems are more challenging for students. Upon first reading, the path to a solution is not immediately evident. Students draw on a bank of strategies (teacher-presented and student-developed) to solve the problem. Possible strategies include

1. Act it out/use materials.
2. Draw a picture/diagram.
3. Look for a pattern.
4. Use logical reasoning.
5. Guess and check.
6. Make an organized list.
7. Make a table.
8. Work backwards.
9. Use an equation.
10. Use simpler numbers.

Some non-routine problem-solving strategies are more appropriate for use at specific grade levels than others. The chart below provides details about when each strategy is addressed in the *Hands-On Problem-Solving* program:

Strategy	Grade 1	Grade 2	Grade 3	Grade 4	Grade 5	Grade 6	Grade 7	Grade 8
Act it out/use materials	✓	✓	✓	✓	✓	✓	✓	✓
Draw a picture/diagram	✓	✓	✓	✓	✓	✓	✓	✓
Look for a pattern	✓	✓	✓	✓	✓	✓	✓	✓
Use logical reasoning	✓	✓	✓	✓	✓	✓	✓	✓
Guess and check		✓	✓	✓	✓	✓	✓	✓
Make an organized list		✓	✓	✓	✓	✓	✓	✓
Make a table			✓	✓	✓	✓	✓	✓
Work backwards					✓	✓	✓	✓
Use an equation					✓	✓	✓	✓
Use simpler numbers					✓	✓	✓	✓

Descriptions of these strategies are provided in detail in the Implementation of Non-Routine Problems section (see page 124).

Extended Exploration Problems

Extended exploration problems are meant to provide a thought-provoking challenge for students. These problems may present mathematical situations that are slightly beyond the grade-level curricular outcomes/expectations, may take the form of an investigation, or may require an extended period of time to solve. In all cases, students are encouraged to use their own strategies to arrive at (a) solution(s).

Extended exploration problems are open ended, can be investigative in nature, and have multiple entry points to allow for differentiation. They often

- Have more than one solution/answer
- Can be solved using a variety of strategies
- Require students to gather their own data
- Require creative and critical thinking
- Require more/extended time to solve
- Make connections to the real world.

Extended exploration problems support the other six "big idea" mathematical processes: communication, connections, mental math, estimation, reasoning, technology, and visualization. The engaging nature of these problems helps students develop perseverance and critical thinking.

Examples and procedures for extended explorations are described in detail in the Implementation of Extended Exploration Problems section (see page 214).

Implementing the Hands-On Problem-Solving Program

Hands-On Problem Solving is arranged in a format that makes it easy for teachers to plan and implement, with tasks that relate to specific outcomes/learning expectations established in Canadian curriculum documents.

Program Format

Problem-solving tasks are presented as daily mathematics activities and are organized according to the approximate number of weeks in the school year. As such, there are 40 weeks-worth of problem-solving tasks, consisting of

- 40 routine problems that focus on math topics including number, patterns, measurement, and geometry. These problems are identified as problems 1A through 40A.

- 40 non-routine problems that focus on specific strategies for the grade level. These problems are identified as problems 1B through 40B.

- 10 extended explorations that offer in-depth, real-life contexts as the basis for problem solving. These problems are identified as problems 1C through 10C.

Planning Your Year of Problem Solving

The three types of problems (routine, non-routine, and extended explorations) are presented in three separate sections of this book, each with its own detailed introduction on implementation. However, it is essential that students focus on all three types of problems throughout the school year. Therefore, it is recommended that teachers do one routine and one non-routine routine problem with students each week, and one extended exploration each month.

Introduction

In the following section of **Hands-On Problem Solving** a correlation chart identifies the math concepts presented in each lesson of the book. Teachers can refer to this chart to plan problem-solving activities that correspond with other math activities occurring in the classroom. For example, if students are focusing on 2-D shapes in math, the correlation chart will show which problems herein connect to that topic.

Curricular Connections

Efforts have been made to correlate **Hands-On Problem-Solving** problems with other curricular areas, such as language arts, science, and social studies. For example, children's literature is referenced in some problems to provide a context. Other problems connect specifically to a science or social studies topic or to a general area of emphasis such as social justice. As teachers become familiar with the problems, they will find opportunities to connect these problems to specific units or topics of study.

Supporting Literacy During Problem Solving

To support beginning grade 1 students, many of whom will be emerging readers, activity sheets for the first 13 routine and non-routine problems are presented in rebus format, meaning that some words are displayed with pictorial representations. These illustrations, however, are not displayed on the corresponding lesson plans for teachers.

It is important that all students, regardless of reading ability, have the opportunity to participate and succeed in problem solving. As such, some will require additional supports to read and understand the problems presented. To help support students' literacy skills, consider the following options:

- Read the problem aloud, and have students follow along.
- Read the problem as a class.
- Have students work with partners or in small groups to read and discuss the problem.
- Introduce, discuss, and review related math vocabulary, and display pictorial representations in the classroom (for example, display labelled illustrations of triangles, squares, and rectangles during a lesson in which students must draw on knowledge of 2-D shapes).

The Questioning Process

During the problem-solving process, it is important for teachers and students to pose questions and to consider various strategies for solving the problem. To encourage these processes, blackline masters of guiding questions have been included for teacher and student use (see page 10). These two templates (one for teacher use and the other for student use) provide suggested questions that can be asked during the problem-solving process.

The blackline masters can be photocopied onto sturdy tag board and laminated for long-term use. Teachers may choose to use these resources during lessons, as they support students in their problem solving. Students can glue their cards into problem-solving file folders or notebooks, or the cards can be placed on desks or tables for use during problem-solving activities.

Additional Resources

For some problem-solving tasks, students might use strategies requiring specific materials, such as hundred charts, number lines, graph paper, dot paper, and so on. These materials can be found in the Appendix at the back of the **Hands-On Problem-Solving** book (see page 243); teachers are encouraged to photocopy these resources and distribute them to students as needed.

▶

A Note About Pennies

The Government of Canada, in its 2012 Budget, announced its intention to withdraw the Canadian penny from circulation; as of fall 2012 the Royal Canadian Mint will no longer distribute pennies. However, the Government of Canada has also indicated that

- The penny will remain Canada's smallest unit for pricing of goods and services.
- The penny will retain its value indefinitely, and consumers can continue to use it in payments for goods and services.

Government of Canada Budget 2012 – Eliminating the Penny <www.budget.gc.ca/2012/themes/theme2-eng.html>

Pennies are still included in some problems in the **Hands-On Problem-Solving** program. The rationale is that using pennies in a problem-solving context

- Supports counting skills
- Builds familiarity with money
- Lends itself to grouping and place-value structure of base ten
- Prepares students for global citizenship. Many monetary systems still include a penny or other coin with a value of 1.
- Can extend to opportunities to explore other Canadian coins that are in circulation but may not be used on a regular basis (for example, the 50-cent coin).

Blackline Masters to Guide and Support Learning – Problem Solving

Guiding Questions for Problem Solving (Teacher Template)

- What do you need to find out?
- What information is important in the problem?
- What information is not important?
- Can you name the answer?
- In what ways can the problem be solved?
- What materials can you use to solve the problem?
- What strategies can you use to solve the problem?
- What questions do you have about the problem?

Encourage communication through the use of rich, probing questions and meaningful conversations with and among students.

To Solve the Problem, Ask Myself

- What do I need to find out?
- What is important in the problem?
- What is not important?
- Can I name the answer?
- In what ways can the problem be solved?
- What materials can I use to solve the problem?
- What strategies can I use to solve the problem?
- What questions do I have about the problem?

Mathematics Correlation

The *Hands-On Problem-Solving* series has been designed to complement the mathematics program at any given grade level. Lessons (problems) in this book address the various mathematics topics and concepts focused on in grade 1. The following chart indicates how lessons (problems) in the program connect to these math topics and concepts.

The following correlations are based on an in-depth review of mathematics curriculum documents from across Canada, including the Western/Northern Canadian Protocol (WNCP), Ontario, and Atlantic Canada.

Grade 1 Correlation Chart

MATHEMATICS TOPIC	LESSON (PROBLEM) NUMBER
Number	
Counting forward	1A, 17A, 19A, 37A, 1B, 8B, 9B, 10B, 21B, 30B, 31B, 33B, 34B, 36B, 37B, 40B, 1C, 8C
Counting backward	9A, 10A, 11A, 12A, 13A, 24A, 10B, 37B, 39B, 40B
Subitizing	16A
Counting on	1A, 7A, 8A, 17A, 19A, 24A, 37A, 1B, 9B, 31B, 40B
Skip counting by 2s	2A, 15A, 18A, 19A, 29A, 14B, 6C
Skip counting by 5s	3A, 16A, 17A, 23A, 10B
Skip counting By 10s	4A, 26A
Comparing sets	5A, 6A, 12A, 13A, 15A, 22A, 23A, 25A, 2B, 3B
Part-part-whole relationships	6A, 10A, 11A, 12A, 16A
Equal groups	2A, 3A, 4A, 18A, 23A, 25A, 3B, 4B, 5B, 8B, 10B, 22B, 25B, 28B, 30B, 32B, 34B, 1C, 3C, 5C, 6C
+1 −1 +2 −2	14A, 23B
Screened tasks	12A, 13A
Operations	
Addition	1A, 2A, 3A, 4A, 6A, 7A, 8A, 15A, 16A, 17A, 18A, 19A, 21A, 22A, 23A, 24A, 25A, 27A, 29A, 37A, 1B, 9B, 21B, 22B, 23B, 25B, 26B, 28B, 30B, 31B, 34B, 37B, 40B, 1C, 2C, 4C, 6C, 7C, 10C
Subtraction	9A, 10A, 11A, 12A, 13A, 15A, 20A, 24A, 23B, 37B, 40B, 10C
Mental math	1A, 7A, 8A, 9A, 10A, 11A, 12A, 13A, 14A, 15A, 29A, 15B, 2C
Patterns and Relations	
Recognizing patterns	13B, 14B, 15B, 21B, 28B, 33B, 36B, 39B, 3C
Repeating patterns	30A, 31A, 32A, 11B, 12B, 13B, 15B, 21B, 24B, 26B, 3C
Equality	28A, 4C

Introduction

Measurement	
Length	34A, 8C
Area	33A
Mass	35A
Geometry	
2-D shapes	36A, 37A, 38A, 7B, 15B, 16B, 24B, 9C
3-D objects	39A, 9C
2-D shapes and 3-D objects	37A, 40A, 16B, 9C

The Hands-On Problem Solving Assessment Plan

Hands-On Problem Solving provides a variety of assessment tools that enables teachers to build a comprehensive and authentic daily assessment plan for their students. Current research identifies the value of quality classroom assessment and the importance of gathering a variety of assessment data, including products, observation of process, and conversation (Davies 2011). For these purposes, suggestions are provided throughout **Hands-On Problem Solving** for authentic classroom-based assessment, including *assessment for learning, assessment as learning,* and *assessment of learning.*

It is important to keep in mind that these are merely suggestions. Teachers are encouraged to use the assessment strategies presented in a wide variety of ways, and also to bring in their own valuable experience as educators to build an effective assessment plan.

Assessment for Learning

It is essential to assess student understanding before, during and after a problem-solving lesson. The information gathered from this formative assessment helps teachers determine students' needs and then plan the next steps in instruction.

To assess students as they work, teachers may choose to use the assessment-for-learning suggestions and questions offered with many lessons (problems). Questions focus on the lesson outcomes/expectations and promote higher-level thinking skills, active inquiry, and decision making.

While observing and conversing with students, teachers may elect to use the Anecdotal Record sheet as well as the Individual Student Observations sheet to record assessment-for-learning data:

- **Anecdotal Record**: To gain an authentic view of a student's progress, it is critical to record observations *during* problem-solving activities. The Anecdotal Record sheet, included on page 16, provides teachers with a format for recording individual or group observations.

- **Individual Student Observations**: For activities during which they would like to focus more on individual students for longer periods of time, teachers may consider using the Individual Student Observations sheet, found on page 17. This blackline master provides more space for comments and is especially useful during conferencing, interviews, or individual student performance tasks.

Assessment as Learning

It is also important for students to reflect on their own learning in relation to problem solving. Student self-reflection and self-assessment empowers students to think more deeply about the way they learn, the strategies they use, the progress they are making, and the adjustments they need to make to extend their learning.

For the purpose of assessment as learning, teachers may choose to use the **Student Self-Assessment** sheet included on page 18. This sheet encourages students to reflect on what they have accomplished, their successes and challenges, and how they can extend their learning.

In addition, a **Problem-Solving Journal** sheet, found on page 19, will encourage students to reflect on their own learning. Teachers can photocopy several journal sheets for each student, cut them in half, add a cover, and bind the sheets together. Students can then create title pages for their own journals. For variety, teachers may also have students use the blank

▶

backsides of each page for more reflections. For example, have students draw or write about

- New problem-solving challenges
- Favourite problem-solving activities
- Real-life experiences with problem solving
- New problem-solving terminology.

For beginning readers and writers, teachers may read the text on the Student Self-Assessment sheet and the Problem-Solving Journal sheet to students. In addition, teachers may help students by recording their responses in order not to restrict their ideas. As students' reading and writing skills develop, teachers may provide them with guidance in completing these sheets independently, through modelling or peer support, and encourage them to progress toward independence.

Student reflections can also be captured in many ways other than in writing. For example, students can

- Interview one another to share their reflections on the problem-solving process
- Write an outline or brief script and make a video reflection
- Create a PowerPoint slide with an audio-recording of their reflections.

Assessment of Learning

Assessment of learning provides a summary of student progress related to the accomplishment of curricular outcomes or expectations at a particular point in time. It is important to gather a variety of assessment data to draw conclusions about what a student knows and can do. Consider collecting student work, observing their learning processes, and having conversations with them for evaluation purposes.

Assessment of learning suggestions are provided throughout the *Hands-On Problem-Solving* program. Use copies of the Anecdotal Record sheet, found on page 16, and the **Individual Student Observations** sheet, found on page 17, to record your assessment-of-learning observations.

Performance Assessment

Performance assessment is planned, systematic observation and assessment based on students actually doing a specific activity (in this case, a problem-solving task). Teacher- or teacher/student-created **Rubrics** can be used to assess student performance on a given problem solving task.

A sample Rubric and a blackline master for teacher use are included on pages 20 and 21. For any specific activity, discuss with students criteria for completing a task successfully. Then, select four criteria that relate directly to the learning outcomes or expectations, and record these criteria on the Rubric. Students receive a checkmark for each criterion accomplished, to determine a Rubric score from a total of four marks. The Rubric scores can then be transferred to the **Rubric Class Record** sheet found on page 22.

Note: Performance tasks can be used for both assessment *for* learning and assessment *of* learning.

Portfolios

A portfolio is a collection of work that shows evidence of a student's learning. Teachers can use the portfolio to reflect the student's progress in problem solving over the course of the school year. Select, with student input, work to include in a problem-solving portfolio or in a problem-solving section of a mathematics or multi-subject portfolio. This should include

▶

representative samples of student work in all types of problem solving. Blackline masters are included to organize students' portfolios (a **Portfolio Table of Contents** sheet is included on page 23, and a **Portfolio Entry Record** sheet is included on page 24).

Date: _____

Anecdotal Record

Purpose of Observation: _____

Student/Group	Student/Group
Comments	Comments
Student/Group	Student/Group
Comments	Comments
Student/Group	Student/Group
Comments	Comments

Date: _____

Individual Student Observations

Purpose of Observation: _____

Student: _____
Observations
Student: _____
Observations
Student: _____
Observations

Date: _____   Name: _____

Student Self-Assessment

Looking at My Problem Solving

1. What I did in problem solving: _____

_____

_____

2. I learned: _____

_____

_____

3. I did very well at: _____

_____

_____

4. I would like to learn more about: _____

_____

_____

5. One thing I like about solving problems is: _____

_____

_____

Date: _____

Problem-Solving Journal

Date: _____   Name: _____

Today in problem solving, I _____ (describe activity)

_____

I learned _____

_____

I would like to learn more about _____

_____

Name: _____

Problem-Solving Journal

Date: _____   Name: _____

Today in problem solving, I _____ (describe activity)

_____

I learned _____

_____

I would like to learn more about _____

_____

19

Sample Rubric

Problem-Solving Activity: Sorting 3-D Objects

Problem-Solving Topic: Geometry

Date: October 12

	4 – Full Accomplishment
	3 – Substantial Accomplishment
	2 – Partial Accomplishment
	1 – Little Accomplishment

Student	Criteria			Rubric Score /4
	Builds a structure using 8 or more 3-D objects	Sorts the 3-D objects into groups	Explains sorting rules	Identifies 2-D shapes on the 3-D objects	
Eli	✓		✓	✓	3
Chris	✓	✓	✓	✓	4

Rubric

Problem-Solving Activity: _____

Problem-Solving Topic: _____

Date: _____

	4 – Full Accomplishment
	3 – Substantial Accomplishment
	2 – Partial Accomplishment
	1 – Little Accomplishment

Student	Criteria			Rubric Score /4

Teacher: _____

Rubric Class Record

Student	Module/Activity/Date								
	Rubric Scores /4								

Scores on Specific Tasks	Assessment
1	Little Accomplishment
2	Partial Accomplishment
3	Substantial Accomplishment
4	Full Accomplishment

Date: _____   Name: _____

Portfolio Table of Contents

Entry   **Date**   **Selection**

1. _____   _____
2. _____   _____
3. _____   _____
4. _____   _____
5. _____   _____
6. _____   _____
7. _____   _____
8. _____   _____
9. _____   _____
10. _____   _____
11. _____   _____
12. _____   _____
13. _____   _____
14. _____   _____
15. _____   _____
16. _____   _____
17. _____   _____
18. _____   _____
19. _____   _____
20. _____   _____

Date: _____   Name: _____

Portfolio Entry Record

This work was chosen by _____

This work is _____

_____

I chose this work because _____

_____

_____

_____

_____

Note: The student may complete this form, or the teacher can scribe for the student.

Date: _____   Name: _____

Portfolio Entry Record

This work was chosen by _____

This work is _____

_____

I chose this work because _____

_____

_____

_____

_____

Note: The student may complete this form, or the teacher can scribe for the student.

Routine Problems

Implementation of Routine Problems

Routine problems are problems in which the way to a solution is generally straightforward. The solution usually involves one or two arithmetic operations.

Problem Types

Efforts are made to offer a variety of types of routine problems for students to solve in **Hands-On Problem Solving**. As such, those problems focusing on number concepts include the following operations and problem types:

Addition and Subtraction

Beginning Unknown

Routine addition problems in which the first addend is not known, are referred to as *beginning unknown* problems:

□ + 3 = 7

Mary looks out her window and sees 3 birds fly onto the fence.

Now there are 7 birds on the fence.

How many birds were on the fence before Mary looked out her window?

Routine subtraction problems in which the minuend is not known are also referred to as *beginning unknown* problems:

□ − 3 = 7

There are some flowers in the garden.
Joey picks 3 flowers for his dad.
There are 7 flowers left.
How many flowers were there to start?

Middle Unknown

Routine addition problems in which the middle addend is not known are referred to as *middle unknown* problems:

5 + □ = 9

John sees 5 frogs in the pond.

When he looks again there are 9 frogs in the pond.

How many more frogs have come to the pond?

Routine subtraction problems in which the subtrahend is not known are also referred to as *middle unknown* problems:

15 − □ = 9

Charles has 15 pennies in his pocket.

He puts some of them into a donation box at the grocery store.

Now he has 9 pennies left in his pocket.

How many pennies does he put into the donation box?

End Result Unknown

Routine addition problems in which the sum is not known are referred to as *end result unknown* problems:

6 + 9 = □

Jon tries on 6 striped shirts at the department store.

Then he tries on 9 plaid shirts.

How many shirts does he try on all together?

Routine subtraction problems in which the difference is not known are also referred to as *end result unknown* problems:

18 − 4 = □

Jacob has 18 bean plants growing in his garden.

The rabbits eat 4 of the plants.

How many are bean plants are left in the garden?

▶

Multiplication

Product Unknown

Routine multiplication problems in which the product is not known are referred to as *product unknown* problems:

5 x 6 = ☐

For example:

Sasha has 5 bags of oranges.

There are 6 oranges in each bag.

How many oranges does Sasha have altogether?

Martha picks 8 plums.

Jonathan picks 5 times as many plums as Martha.

How many plums does Jonathan pick?

Division

Partitive Division

Routine partitive division problems are problems for which the number of sets (quotient) is known and the total (dividend) is known but how many are in each set (divisor) is not known:

25 ÷ 5 = ☐

For example:

Phil has 25 candies.

He shares them equally among his 5 friends.

How many candies does each friend receive?

Julie has 20 dolls.

She has 4 times as many dolls as Erin.

How many dolls does Erin have?

Quotitive Division

Routine quotitive division problems are problems for which the number in each set (divisor) is known and the total (dividend) is known but how many sets there are (quotient) is not known:

30 ÷ 6 = ☐

For example:

Tarts cost $3 each.

How many tarts can you buy with $15?

Alex buys some oranges for 6 cents each.

He spends a total of 30¢.

How many oranges does he buy?

Teaching Routine Problems

Each routine problem-solving task (lesson plan) provides the following information for teachers:

Math Topic: This specifies the connection to curricular strands, including number, patterns, geometry, measurement, data, probability, and variables and equations.

Math Concepts: This identifies mathematics skills and concepts focused on in the problem, based on the curricular outcomes/expectations.

Problem Type: This identifies the specific problem type, with reference to number operations.

For example

- Beginning, middle, or end result unknown problems for addition and subtraction
- Product unknown problems for multiplication
- Partitive and quotitive problems for division.

Note: Problem type is identified only for problems related to number concepts, and not for problems related to patterns, data, measurement, geometry, and variables and equations. As well, there are some cases in which problems related to number do not require equations or operations to solve, so problem type does not apply to these problems.

Routine Problems

Problem: The problem is stated in grade-appropriate language and reading level.

Background Information for Teachers: In this section, teachers may be provided with guidance regarding basic mathematical knowledge, vocabulary, or skills students will need in order to solve the problem; tips or specific pointers for presenting the problem to students; ideas for scaffolding; and other facts of interest.

This section also includes information on the various strategies students may use to solve a given problem. It is important to encourage diversity and creativity in this area, as there is almost always more than one way to solve a problem!

With some problems, suggestions are provided for materials to help students solve the problem. To promote differentiated instruction and meet the needs of various learners, it is important to provide, as much as possible, any supports that students might need to solve a problem.

For example, some students may choose to use manipulatives, while others may need drawing supplies to draw pictures or writing supplies to record symbols, while others still might use calculators. By predetermining each student's strengths and challenges with mathematical concepts and problem solving, teachers can ensure that students have access to appropriate resources and are encouraged to use strategies that will enable them to succeed at solving routine problems.

Think: Once a problem has been presented to students, it is important to provide some "think" or wait time before asking them to share their ideas. Research suggests that a longer wait time actually increases student engagement (Black et al 2004). In *Hands-On Problem Solving*, this approach is encouraged with the "Think" section, to remind teachers and students to take the time necessary to begin formulating ideas and strategies for solving a problem. Both in teacher lesson plans and on student activity sheets throughout the routine problems, the "Think" step is identified with the icon shown above.

Ensure that adequate time is provided for students to read the problem, identify important information, and think about possible strategies for solving it.

Note: After the third lesson plan, supporting text following the "Think" reminder and icon is omitted, as it would simply repeat from problem to problem.

Talk: The process of communication is an essential element of mathematics and one of the Big Ideas in Mathematics outlined in the Introduction to *Hands-On Problem Solving* (see page 2). Once students have been presented with a problem and provided with time to think about it, the next step is to have them share their ideas, as teachers probe their thinking with critical questions. Suggestions for higher-level questioning are provided in this section. Both in teacher lesson plans and on student activity sheets throughout the routine problems, the "Talk" step is identified with the icon shown below, left.

Note: These questions are provided for guidance and scaffolding. However, teachers may not find it necessary to ask all of the questions with every problem. At the same time, teachers may find that questions are necessary to provide support to some students, while others can move ahead to solve the problem independently. Questions should be posed at the teacher's discretion and are not necessarily required with each problem and for every student.

Encouraging students to ask questions is also a critical component of the "Talk" step. Engage students in such dialogue by regularly asking:

- What questions do you have about the problem?//
- Is there a question you would like to ask me (the teacher) or your classmates?

The talking stage of the problem-solving process is also a time to have students:

- **Identify important information in the problem:** Encourage students to point out any essential facts in a word problem. For example, for the following problem, important information is shown in bold text:

  Jinan and Tegan are collecting cans of soup for a local soup kitchen. They collect soup cans for 5 days. **Jinan collects 13 cans of soup, and Tegan collects 9 cans.** How many cans of soup do they donate to the soup kitchen?

  Students may use highlighters to mark this information or use coloured pencils to circle important words.

- **Identify unimportant or extraneous information in the problem:** Many problems present information that is not required in order to solve a problem. This kind of information can distract students from focusing on essential information and can therefore influence their success in solving the problem. It is important for students to identify the information that can be considered non-essential to the problem-solving task at hand. For example, using the same problem as before, the non-essential information is underlined:

  Jinan and Tegan are collecting cans of soup for a local soup kitchen. They collect soup cans for 5 days. **Jinan collects 13 cans of soup, and Tegan collects 9 cans.** How many cans of soup do they donate to the soup kitchen?

  Students may use a pencil to underline the unimportant information in a problem.

- **Name the answer:** It is important for students to be able to identify and articulate what it is they are attempting to find out. For example, if asked to name the answer for the preceding problem, the response should be "cans of soup."

- **Share possible strategies:** Encourage students to talk about various ways to approach a problem, including the use of manipulatives, pictures, symbols, and calculators, as well as any personal strategies they have. This is a time and place to encourage risk-taking and the sharing of new ideas!

During the "Talk" stage of the problem-solving process, it is important that students *not* share possible *solutions* to the problem and instead discuss only the process and strategies.

It can also be beneficial for teachers to engage students in talk during the problem-solving process. For example, students may be asked or told:

- What do you notice?
- Are there any challenges that we need to discuss?
- Take a walk about, and discuss your work with other students. Ask questions of each other.

This process helps to build a community of learners.

Routine Problems

Note: Because the "Talk" process is relatively consistent from problem to problem, supporting text following the "Talk" reminder and icon is included only with the first three routine problems. With the fourth lesson plan and onward, the "Talk" reminder and icon alone serve as cues for teachers and students, who will by now be familiar with the process. Remember to refer to the support card templates on page 10 for questions to guide the Talk stage.

Solve: In this section of each teacher lesson plan, the correct response to the problem is provided. Students are expected to record their answer to the problem in the "Solve" section on the corresponding activity sheet. Have students record their strategies and provide solutions, being sure to also name their answer. Both in teacher lesson plans and on student activity sheets throughout the routine problems, the "Solve" step is identified with the icon shown above.

For the soup can problem, students' solutions might include

1. Using manipulatives, such as counters:

2. Drawing pictures:

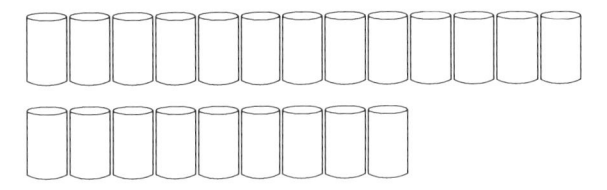

3. Using an empty number line:

4. Using a hundred chart (start at 13, add 10, subtract 1):

1	2	3	4	5	6	7	8	9	10
11	12	13	14	15	16	17	18	19	20
21	22	23	24	25	26	27	28	29	30
31	32	33	34	35	36	37	38	39	40
41	42	43	44	45	46	47	48	49	50
51	52	53	54	55	56	57	58	59	60
61	62	63	64	65	66	67	68	69	70
71	72	73	74	75	76	77	78	79	80
81	82	83	84	85	86	87	88	89	90
91	92	93	94	95	96	97	98	99	100

5. Using a number line (find 13, and count on 9):

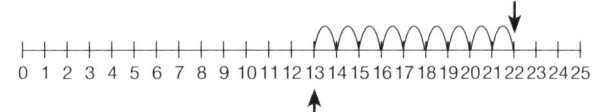

6. Using a number sentence or equation:

   $13 + 9 = 22$

Share: Students should be given time to share their strategies and solutions with their teacher and classmates. This is an integral part of learning problem-solving skills, as students learn new strategies from one another. Honouring students' responses, whether right or wrong, can lead to opportunities for healthy mathematical discussions that create a learning environment where all can feel they have a voice and can take risks as learners. The role of the teacher as faciltator is crucial during this sharing session to ensure that each student's mathematical understanding is progressing and that misconceptions are not perpetuated.

Both in teacher lesson plans and on student activity sheets throughout the routine problems, the "Share" step is identified with the icon shown on page 30.

Note: After the third lesson plan, supporting text following the "Share" reminder and icon is omitted, as it would simply repeat from problem to problem.

Extend: Suggestions for extension activities appear only on the teacher lesson plans and not on the corresponding student activity sheets. Extending the problem-solving experience allows students to further develop communication skills and challenge their mathematical thinking. For each problem, teachers are provided with suggestions for additional related activities or tasks, such as solving a related problem, writing about the problem, creating a similar problem, showing the solution in more than one way (for example, adding a pictorial representation to a recorded answer, or adding a word answer to a numerical one), and so on. Of course, teachers are also encouraged to conduct other extension activities based on their own wealth of ideas and experience.

Assessment *for*, *as*, and *of* Learning: Assessment suggestions appear on some of the teacher lesson plans but not on the corresponding student activity sheets. Based on current research about the value of quality classroom assessment (Davies 2011), suggestions are provided for authentic assessment, which includes assessment *for* learning, assessment *as* learning, and assessment *of* learning. These assessment strategies focus specifically on the learning outcomes that are related to a particular problem-solving task.

Keep in mind that these suggestions are merely ideas to consider; teachers are also encouraged to use their own assessment techniques and to refer to the other assessment strategies outlined in detail in the Assessment section of **Hands-On Problem Solving** on pages 13 to 24.

Routine Problem Solving Activity Sheet: A corresponding student activity sheet correlates with each problem-solving task provided in the teacher lesson plan. Each activity sheet supports students in the problem-solving process by presenting the problem followed by the guiding cues ("Think", "Talk", "Solve", and "Share") and matching picture icons. There is also space for students to show their solving strategies.

Students may work independently on these activity sheets, with partners or in small groups, or teachers may choose to read through the problems together with students and to complete them in large group settings. Activity sheets can also be made into overheads, projected onto a screen using a document camera, or recreated on chart paper.

Student completion of the activity sheets fosters development of communication skills in mathematics and can also be used as evidence of essential learning related to the problem-solving process.

Routine Problems

1A Cole Finds Seashells

Math Topic

Number

Math Concepts

- Counting on
- Addition

Problem Type

Addition: End result unknown (a + b = ?)

Problem

Cole is at the beach.

He finds 5 seashells.

He walks down the beach.

He finds 4 more seashells.

How many seashells does Cole find?

Background Information for Teachers

At the beginning of grade 1, students should be provided with numerous opportunities to build number concepts through manipulation of materials, counting objects, matching, and comparing sets. As students explore the following rebus problems, they should begin to verbalize the number sentence or story orally before they are introduced to symbols and equations.

Students may use a variety of strategies to solve this problem, such as the following:

- Use manipulatives to act out the problem.
- Use counters to match pictures onto the rebus story.
- Draw a picture, and count on.

Students should have access to math materials (manipulatives, counters, or drawing materials) at all times to allow them to implement a chosen strategy.

Think

Provide time for students to read, think, and formulate ideas about the problem.

Talk

Discuss the problem with students. Ask:

- What do you need to find out? (how many seashells Cole finds)
- What is important in the problem? (Have students use coloured pencils or markers to highlight or circle the important information, or model this for them.)
- What is not important? (Have students use pencils to underline the unimportant information, or model this for them.)
- Can you name the answer? (seashells)
- How can you solve the problem?
- What materials can you use to solve the problem?
- What strategies can you use to solve the problem?

Discuss the problem as a class, in small groups, or in pairs. Encourage communication through the use of rich, probing questions and meaningful conversations with and among students. Be sure to have students share their ideas about the materials and strategies they could use to help them solve the problem. Encourage students to ask questions as well.

Solve

Cole finds 9 seashells.

Share

Have students share their strategies and solutions.

1A

Extend

Have students bring seashell collections from home (or pick some up at a craft or dollar store). Challenge students to use the shells to create their own story problems. Problems can be acted out for the class and solved as a group.

Routine Problems

Date: _____ Name: _____

Cole Finds Seashells

Cole is at the beach.

He finds 5 seashells.

He walks down the beach.

He finds 4 more seashells.

How many seashells does Cole find?

Think

Talk

Solve

Share

2A | Jake Has Goldfish

Math Topic
Number

Math Concepts
- Counting by 2s
- Addition

Problem Type
Addition: End result unknown (a + b = ?)

Problem
Jake has a bowl of goldfish.

He has 6 goldfish.

How many eyes are there on all 6 goldfish?

Background Information for Teachers

Although they may use addition to solve this problem, students will likely focus on their counting skills, specifically counting by 2s. Some students may also count using one-to-one correspondence. To scaffold the problem and focus on counting by 2s, have students work in small groups of three to five students, and challenge them to count how many ears they have altogether. Vary the size of the groups, and have students count hands, feet, elbows, and so on.

Students may use a variety of strategies to solve this problem, such as the following:

- Use manipulatives to act out the problem.
- Use counters to match pictures onto the rebus story.
- Draw a picture, and count.
- Count by 2s orally.

Think

Talk

Discuss the problem with students. Ask:

- What do you need to find out? (how many eyes on all 6 goldfish)
- What is important in the problem? (Have students use coloured pencils or markers to highlight or circle the important information, or model this for them.)
- What is not important? (Have students use pencils to underline the unimportant information, or model this for them.)
- Can you name the answer? (eyes)
- How can you solve the problem?
- What materials can you use to solve the problem?
- What strategies can you use to solve the problem?

Discuss the problem as a class, in small groups, or in pairs. Encourage communication through the use of rich, probing questions and meaningful conversations with and among students. Be sure to have students share their ideas about the materials and strategies they could use to help them solve the problem. Encourage students to ask questions as well.

Solve
There are 12 eyes on the fish.

Share

Extend

Provide students with the following extension problem:

If Jake gets 3 more fish for his birthday, how many fish does he have now?

How many eyes are there on all Jake's fish?

Routine Problems

Date: _____   Name: _____

Jake Has Goldfish

Jake has a bowl of goldfish.

He has 6 goldfish

How many eyes are there on all 6 goldfish?

Think

Talk

Solve

Share

36   2A

3A | Mrs. Kahn's Students Take the Bus

Math Topic

Number

Math Concepts

- Counting by 5s
- Addition

Problem Type

Addition: End result unknown (a + b = ?)

Problem

Mrs. Khan is a grade one teacher.

She asks her students, "Who took the bus to school today?"

4 students raise their hands.

How many fingers are raised?

Background Information for Teachers

Although they may use addition to solve this problem, students will likely focus on their counting skills, specifically counting by 5s.

Note: Ensure that students understand they should count the thumb as a finger for this problem.

Students may use a variety of strategies to solve this problem, such as the following:

- Use manipulatives to act out the problem.
- Use counters to match pictures onto the rebus story.
- Draw a picture, and count.
- Count by 5s orally.

Think

Talk

Discuss the problem as a class, in small groups, or in pairs. Pose questions (as outlined on the support cards—see page 10), and encourage students to ask questions as well.

Solve

20 fingers are raised

Share

Extend

- Provide students with this extension problem:

    How many students in your class take the bus to school?

    If each of these students raises a hand, how many fingers will be raised?

    Have students raise their hands if they take the bus, and count the fingers by 5s.

- Extend the task further to determine how many students walk or are driven to school by car. Have students raise their hands accordingly, and then count these fingers as well.

Routine Problems

Mrs. Kahn's Students Take the Bus

Mrs. Khan is a grade one teacher.

She asks her students, "Who took the bus to school today?"

4 students raise their hands.

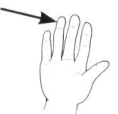

How many fingers are raised?

Think

Talk

Solve

Share

4A Charlie Makes Pattern Trains

Math Topic

Number

Math Concepts

- Counting by 10s
- Addition

Problem Type

Addition: End result unknown (a + b = ?)

Problem

Charlie is making pattern trains with cubes.

Each pattern train he makes has 10 cubes.

He makes 5 pattern trains altogether.

How many cubes does Charlie use?

Background Information for Teachers

Students may use a variety of strategies to solve this problem, such as the following:

- Use manipulatives, such as interlocking cubes, to make pattern trains, and act out the problem.
- Use counters to match pictures on the rebus story.
- Count by 10s orally.

Assessment for Learning

Before students attempt to solve this problem, observe, and determine their ability to use manipulatives to

- Count by 1s in a forward number sequence
- Count and create sets of 10
- Create 10-cube pattern trains.

Use the Anecdotal Record sheet included on page 16 to record results.

Think

Talk

Solve

Charlie uses 50 cubes altogether

Share

Extend

- Present the following extension problem to students:

    If Charlie has 30 more cubes, how many more pattern trains can he make?

- As a further extension, provide students with interlocking cubes, and have them create their own story problems.

Routine Problems

Date: _____   Name: _____

Charlie Makes Pattern Trains

Charlie is making pattern trains with cubes.

Each pattern train he makes has 10 cubes.

He makes 5 pattern trains altogether.

How many cubes does Charlie use?

Think

Talk

Solve

Share

5A Cheyenne Recycles Juice Boxes

Math Topic

Number

Math Concept

Comparing sets

Problem

Cheyenne is collecting juice boxes to recycle.

She has orange juice boxes. (14 boxes shown)

She also has apple juice boxes. (11 boxes shown)

Which set has less?

Background Information for Teachers

Students need many opportunities to count and compare sets, using terms such as *same, more,* and *fewer*. To scaffold this problem, provide students with counters, and conduct several activities that involve comparing sets. For example:

- Make a set of 10 counters.
- Make another set with fewer counters.
- Make 2 sets with the same number of counters.
- Make another set with more counters.

As students do these tasks, encourage them to use the terms *more, less,* and *same,* to compare their own sets as well as to compare the sets other students make with their own.

Students may use a variety of strategies to solve this problem, such as the following:

- Use manipulatives, such as cubes, to represent the juice boxes, and act out the problem.
- Use counters to match pictures onto the rebus story.
- Use cubes and a balance scale to compare the sets.

Think

Talk

Solve

The set of apple-juice boxes has less.

Share

Extend

- Provide students with the following extension problem:

    Cheyenne also collects peach-juice boxes.

    She has more peach juice boxes than orange juice boxes.

    Draw or build a set to show how many peach juice boxes Cheyenne might have.

- As an additional extension, have students use interlocking cubes and balance scales to explore building sets according to the concepts of *same, more,* and *fewer*. This approach enables students to kinesthetically and visually investigate and apply concepts related to comparing sets.

Routine Problems

Date: _____   Name: _____

Cheyenne Recycles Juice Boxes

Cheyenne is collecting juice boxes to recycle.

She has orange juice boxes.

She also has apple juice boxes.

Which set has less?

Think

Talk

Solve

Share

5A

6A | Lester Has Jellybeans

Math Topic

Number

Math Concepts

- Part-part-whole relationships
- Addition

Problem

Lester has a handful of jellybeans.

He has 5 jellybeans altogether.

Some jellybeans are red, and some jellybeans are black.

How many of each colour might Lester have?

Background Information for Teachers

This problem provides an opportunity for students to explore part-part-whole relationships, which involves seeing numbers as made up of two or more parts. After students learn to count, they need to work on part-part-whole relationships in order to build an understanding of the processes of addition and subtraction. For example, if students are working on the number 5, they may

- Use 2 colours of counters to make various sets equaling 5
- Place 5 two-sided, two-coloured counters in a bag, shake them out, and count the number of each colour
- String beads or make interlocking-cube trains of 5 using two different colours.

Students will benefit from investigating part-part-whole relationships as a foundation for the concepts of addition and subtraction.

Students may use a variety of strategies to solve this problem, such as the following:

- Use manipulatives, such as red and black jellybeans.
- Draw pictures of the possible combinations.
- String 5 beads of two different colours to represent the possible combinations.
- Create pattern trains with two different colours of interlocking cubes.

Think

Talk

Solve

Lester could have

1 red and 4 black jellybeans	or
2 red and 3 black jellybeans	or
3 red and 2 black jellybeans	or
4 red and 1 black jellybeans.	

Share

Extend

- Have students depict this problem pictorially. On construction paper, have them trace a hand (students may trace their own hands or a partner's hand) and then draw and colour 5 jellybeans in the hand red or black. Encourage students to create all possible combinations.

- As an additional extension, have students play "Cube Snap". First, ask students to build a train of 5 interlocking cubes. Then, have students snap apart the cubes to make two smaller trains, observing and identifying the part-part-whole relationships:

  5 is the same as 2 and 3.

  As students build conceptual understanding and confidence they can play this game with increasing numbers to 10.

Note: As subsequent problems are presented, continue to explore part-part-whole relationships with the various numbers involved.

Routine Problems

Lester Has Jellybeans

Lester has a handful of jellybeans.

He has 5 jellybeans altogether.

Some jellybeans are red, and some jellybeans are black.

How many of each colour might Lester have?

Think

Talk

Solve

Share

7A | Jan and Bob See Birds

Math Topic

Number

Math Concepts

- Addition
- Counting on

Problem Type

Addition: End result unknown (a + b = ?)

Problem

Jan and Bob go to the forest.

Jan sees 4 birds in a tree.

Bob sees 2 birds on the grass.

How many birds do Bob and Jan see altogether?

Background Information for Teachers

It is important to continue to encourage students to build a deep understanding of number by continuing to use concrete and pictorial representations.

Students may use a variety of strategies to solve this problem, such as the following:

- Draw a picture, and count on.
- Use manipulatives to act out the problem.
- Use a beaded frame card (shown below. To create, use thick cardboard or picture matte; punch two holes on each end; string beads onto pipe cleaners; put pipe cleaners through holes, and attach with tape). Ready-made frames, called addition racks or *rekenreks*, are also available. Students can use the beaded frames to add and subtract numbers to 20 and to explore part-part-whole combinations.

Note: Students should have access to math materials at all times to allow them to implement a chosen strategy.

Think

Talk

Solve

Bob and Jan see 6 birds altogether.

Share

Extend

Have students use beaded frame cards, manipulatives, or draw pictures to represent numbers and create their own oral problems. For example:

There are _____ _____ .
           (e.g., 6)   (e.g., spiders)

_____ more _____ come.
(e.g., 2)   (e.g., spiders)

How many _____ are there altogether?
            (e.g., spiders)

Have students use the concrete objects and pictorial representations to solve the problems and provide answers in sentence form:

There are _____ _____ altogether.
        (e.g., 8) (e.g., spiders)

Routine Problems

45

Date: _____   Name: _____

Jan and Bob See Birds

Jan and Bob go to the forest.

Jan sees 4 birds in a tree.

Bob sees 2 birds on the grass.

How many birds do Bob and Jan see altogether?

Think

Talk

Solve

Share

7A

8A | Ben Sees Frogs

Math Topic

Number

Math Concepts

- Addition to 20
- Counting on

Problem Type

Addition: End result unknown (a + b = ?)

Problem

Ben is walking by a pond.

He sees 5 frogs on a log.

He sees 3 frogs on a lily pad.

How many frogs does Ben see altogether?

Background Information for Teachers

When students first explore addition, they do so with concrete and pictorial representations, communicating their understanding orally. At these early stages of problem solving using addition, the focus is not on operations or equations. However, as students develop conceptual understanding, mathematical symbols may be introduced. Therefore, as appropriate, introduce the "+" symbol in modeling similar problems. Similarly, students may begin to use equations to represent and communicate solutions.

Note: Using equations is only one strategy in the problem-solving process. Students should still be encouraged to use a variety of other strategies to represent their thinking, including the use of manipulatives, drawings, and so on.

Students may use a variety of strategies to solve this problem, such as the following:

- Draw a picture, and count on.
- Use manipulatives to act out the problem.
- Use a beaded frame card.
- Write an equation: 5 + 3 = 8.

Think

Talk

Solve

Ben sees 8 frogs altogether.

Share

Extend

Provide students with this extension problem:

How many eyes are on the 8 frogs?

Draw a picture to show your answer.

Routine Problems

Date: _____   Name: _____

Ben Sees Frogs

Ben is walking by a pond.

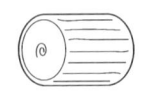

He sees 5 frogs on a log.

He sees 3 frogs on a lily pad.

How many frogs does Ben see altogether?

Think

Talk

Solve

Share

9A | Tammy Sees Squirrels

Math Topic
Number

Math Concepts
- Subtraction
- Counting back

Problem Type
Subtraction: End result unknown (a − b = ?)

Problem
Tammy sees squirrels in her yard.

6 squirrels are in the tree.

2 squirrels run away.

How many squirrels are left in the tree?

Background Information for Teachers

Before subtraction problems are introduced, students need to develop some confidence with backward counting sequences as well as naming numbers before any number to 10. To scaffold this problem, have students participate in the following activities:

- Provide students with 10 objects. Have them count the set, then take away one object at a time as they count backwards from 10 to 0.
- Repeat the preceding activity with sets of any number of objects to 10.
- Have students choose a number between 1 and 10, call it out, and have classmates identify the number before it.

As subtraction problems are introduced, students should be encouraged to use concrete objects and pictorial representations to find solutions.

Students may use a variety of strategies to solve this problem, such as the following:

- Draw a picture, and count back.
- Use manipulatives to act out the problem.
- Use a beaded frame card.

Think

Talk

Solve

There are 4 squirrels left in the tree.

Share

Extend

Use a permanent marker to draw a large ten frame on a plastic shower curtain or vinyl tablecloth, as shown:

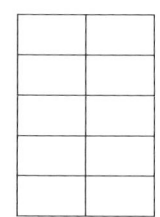

Have students create subtraction problems similar to the one presented, and act them out. For example:

There are 5 squirrels in the yard (5 students stand on the ten-frame, in the squares on the left)

3 squirrels run away (3 students move off the ten-frame)

How many squirrels are left?

Encourage students to position themselves as appropriate on the ten-frame, such that groups of 5 are created first. This helps students to build an understanding of related number concepts. For example, if there are 8 "squirrels", students stand in the 5 squares on the left and then in 3 squares on the right, such that 5 and 3 more is 8.

Routine Problems

Date: _____   Name: _____

Tammy Sees Squirrels

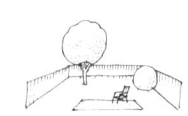

Tammy sees squirrels in her yard.

6 squirrels are in the tree.

2 squirrels run away.

How many squirrels are left in the tree?

Think

Talk

Solve

Share

10A | Max Has a Birthday Cake With Candles

Math Topic
Number

Math Concepts
- Subtraction
- Counting back
- Part-part-whole relationships

Problem Type
Subtraction: End result unknown (a – b = ?)

Problem
Max has a birthday cake.

There are 7 lit candles on the cake.

3 candles go out.

How many candles are still lit?

Background Information for Teachers
Like the preceding problem (9A) this problem provides practice with subtraction.

Students may use a variety of strategies to solve this problem, such as the following:

- Draw a picture, and count back.
- Use manipulatives to act out the problem.
- Use a beaded frame card.

Think

Talk

Solve
There are 4 candles still lit on the cake.

Share

Extend
- Have students create birthday cake pictures and then demonstrate the part-part-whole concept by colouring 7 candles in two different colours.

- To explore different part-part-whole relationships using various numbers, have students create birthday cakes for family members, for older or younger friends, or for characters from a book.

Routine Problems

Max Has a Birthday Cake With Candles

Max has a birthday cake.

There are 7 lit candles on the cake.

3 candles go out.

How many candles are still lit?

Think

Talk

Solve

Share

10A

11A Cookies in a Cookie Jar

Math Topic

Number

Math Concepts

- Subtraction
- Counting back
- Part-part-whole relationships

Problem Type

Subtraction: End result unknown (a – b = ?)

Problem

There are 9 cookies in a cookie jar.

I take 4 cookies out of the cookie jar.

How many cookies are left in the jar?

Background Information for Teachers

To engage students and provide a context for the problem, listen to and sing the song "Who Stole the Cookie from the Cookie Jar" by Sharon, Lois, and Bram. Students may use a variety of strategies to solve this problem, such as the following:

- Draw a picture, and count on.
- Use manipulatives to act out the problem.
- Use a number line to count on.
- Use a beaded frame card.
- Write an equation: 9 – 4 = 5.

Think

Talk

Solve

There are 5 cookies left in the cookie jar.

Share

Extend

Use the Cookie Jar blackline master (included at the end of the lesson on page 55) to support students in solving similar problems. Mount a copy of the cookie-jar BLM onto sturdy tag board, and laminate.

To use this teaching aid, place a sticky note over the box on the cookie jar. When presenting a problem to students, record the answer in the box under the sticky note.

For example:

There are 12 cookies in the cookie jar.

Jack takes out 3 cookies to eat.

How many cookies are left in the jar?

Record the answer (9) in the box under the sticky note. Either record the problem on the back of the cookie jar, or present it orally to students. They can use counters to solve the problem and then confirm their answers by removing the sticky note.

Note: The cookie jar blackline master has potential to be used for various math tasks throughout the school year.

Routine Problems

Date: _____   Name: _____

Cookies in a Cookie Jar

There are 9 cookies in a cookie jar.

I take 4 cookies out of the cookie jar.

How many cookies are left in the jar?

Think

Talk

Solve

Share

Cookie Jar Blackline Master

12A | Bees Go in the Hive

Math Topic
Number

Math Concepts
- Counting a set
- Subtraction
- Counting on
- Counting back
- Part-part-whole relationships
- Screened tasks

Problem Type
Subtraction: End result unknown (a − b = ?)

Problem
_____ bees are flying together.

Some bees go into the empty hive.

The others wait outside.

How many bees go into the hive?

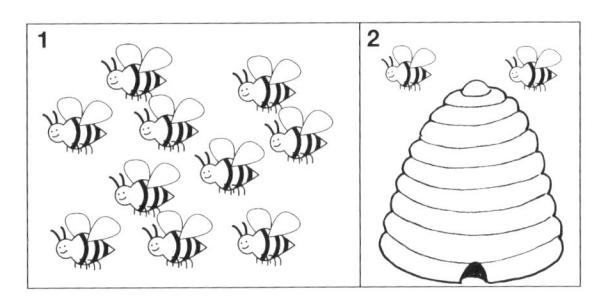

Background Information for Teachers

This problem uses a screened task (a set or portion of a set is hidden). Screened tasks are a key element when working with part-part-whole relationships.

To solve these types of problems students will benefit from experience using manipulatives. A variety of screened tasks with different materials will allow for better understanding.

To preview the problem with students, use a paper bag and counters or interlocking cubes to model similar problem situations. For example:

I have 5 cubes.
I put some in the bag.
There are 2 cubes still in my hand.
How many cubes are in the bag?

In the screened task presented in this lesson, students need to understand that the number of bees has not changed, but some are hidden. Some students may have difficulty with counting the bees. They may devise a strategy that involves marking the bees as they count. Those who are unable to devise a strategy will benefit from discussion of counting strategies during "Talk" time (below).

Students may use a variety of strategies to solve this problem, such as the following:

- Draw a picture, and count on or count back.
- Use manipulatives to act out the problem.
- Use a beaded frame card.
- Write an equation: 10 − 2 = ?

Think

Talk

Solve
There are 8 bees in the hive.

Share

Extend
Have students explore part-part-whole relationships for 10. Provide each student with 10 counters and a container (for example, a margarine tub) to represent the beehive. Pose questions to guide exploration.

12A

For example:

- If there are 3 bees in the hive, how many are outside?
- If there are 5 bees outside the hive, how many are inside?

Explore various set combinations to 10.

Routine Problems

Bees Go in the Hive

_____ bees are flying together.

Some bees go into the empty hive.

The others wait outside.

How many bees go into the hive?

Think

Talk

Solve

Share

12A

13A | Hiding Books Under the Rug

Math Topic

Number

Math Concepts

- Counting a set
- Subtraction
- Counting on
- Counting back
- Screened tasks

Problem Type

Subtraction: End result unknown (a – b =?)

Problem

There were _____ books on the floor.

I hid some of those books under the rug.

_____ books are **not** under the rug.

How many books are under the rug?

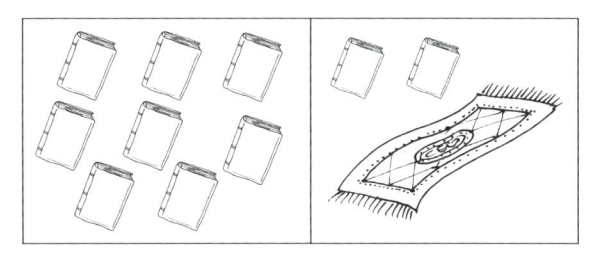

Background Information for Teachers

In this screened task, students should know that the total number of books does not change, but some are hidden. As in previous problems involving counting sets, students may devise a strategy for keeping track of the book count and retaining it.

Students may use a variety of strategies to solve this problem, such as the following:

- Draw a picture, and count on, or count back.
- Use manipulatives to act out the problem.
- Use a beaded frame card.
- Write an equation: 8 – 2 = ?

Think

Talk

Solve

There are 6 books under the rug.

Share

Extend

Use margarine tubs and counters to present more screened tasks for students to solve. Turn each margarine tub upside down, and use a permanent marker to record a number from 5 to 10 on the bottom. Place some counters under the upside-down tub and the remaining counters on top of the tub, to equal the number recorded, as in the example below:

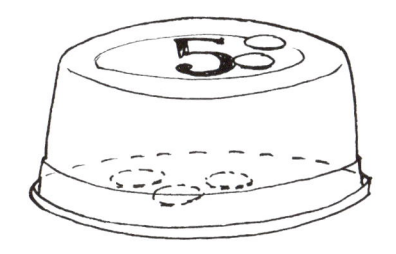

This is an excellent activity to do in pairs or with groups of students, with a different tub and amount of counters on each of several tables in the classroom. Pairs or groups of students can solve the problem and then move to another table.

Note: Screened tasks can be very challenging for students, so it is important to scaffold activities. Begin with combinations of numbers that add up to 5, observe student confidence, and progress accordingly.

Routine Problems

13A

Assessment of Learning

Observe students as they explore the screened tasks presented above, and conference with them individually. Focus on their abilities to use manipulatives (tubs and counters) to determine part-part-whole relationships to 5, and identify their confidence with larger numbers to 10. Record results on a copy of the Individual Student Observations sheet, found on page 17.

Date: _____   Name: _____

Hiding Books Under the Rug

There were _____ books on the floor.

I hid some of those books under the rug.

_____ books are **not** under the rug.

How many books are under the rug?

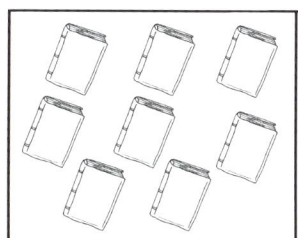

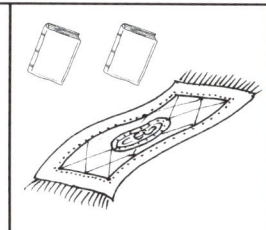

Think

Talk

Solve

Share

13A

14A | Jeffrey Writes a Math Poem

Math Topic
Number

Math Concepts
- Mental math strategies
- Skip counting

Problem

Jeffrey likes to write poems.

He is writing a poem about math.

Fill in the missing numbers.

One more than 15 is _____.
One less than 8 is _____.
One more than 19 is _____.
One less than 12 is _____.

Two more than 13 is _____.
Two less than 10 is _____.
Two more than 16 is _____.
Now, isn't my math great?

Background Information for Teachers

Before students progress to solving addition and subtraction problems with larger numbers, it is important that they build confidence solving problems with 1 more, 1 less, 2 more, and 2 less.

Students may use a variety of strategies to solve this problem, such as the following:

- Use manipulatives, such as counters.
- Use a number line (included in the Appendix on page 244) to determine 1 or 2 more or less.
- Use mental math strategies, such as counting on and counting back.

Think

Talk

Solve

1 more than 15 is **16**.
1 less than 8 is **7**.
1 more than 19 is **20**.
1 less than 12 is **11**.

2 more than 13 is **15**.
2 less than 10 is **8**.
2 more than 16 is **18**.
Now isn't my math great?

Share

Extend

Have students write their own math poems using the 1-more, 1-less, 2-more, 2-less format. Create a class book of students' poems.

Jeffrey Writes a Math Poem

Jeffrey likes to write poems.
He is writing a poem about math.
Fill in the missing numbers:

1 more than 15 is _____.

1 less than 8 is _____.

1 more than 19 is _____.

1 less than 12 is _____.

2 more than 13 is _____.

2 less than 10 is _____.

2 more than 16 is _____.

Now, isn't my math great?

Think

Talk

Solve

Share

15A | Juan Counts Boots and Shoes

Math Topic

Number

Math Concepts

- Counting by 2s, counting by 10s
- Using doubles
- Comparing two sets
- Using an equation

Problem Type

Addition: End result unknown (a + b = ?)

Problem

After recess, Juan looks at all the muddy boots and shoes in the hall.

He sees 5 pairs of boots and 3 pairs of shoes.

How many boots does Juan see?

How many shoes does he see?

Does he see more boots or more shoes?

Background Information for Teachers

For this problem, it is important to clarify information for students, such as the fact that a pair equals 2.

Students may use a variety of strategies to solve this problem, such as the following:

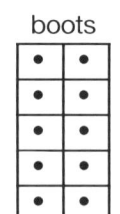

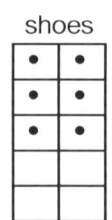

- Draw pictures of boots and shoes.
- Use lined-up interlocking cubes or counters to represent boots and shoes.
- Use a number line (included in the Appendix on page 244) with jumps to represent skip counting by 2s, as in the following example. 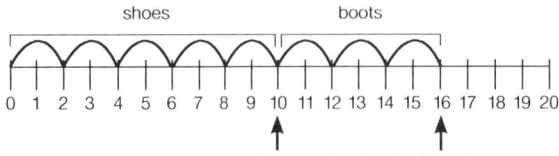
- Use an empty ten frame (included in the Appendix on page 245) with bingo chips to represent boots and shoes, as in the following example.
- Use doubles 5 + 5 = 10; 3 + 3 = 6.

Think

Talk

Solve

There are 10 boots altogether. There are 6 shoes altogether.

Share

Extend

- Extend this problem to measurement tasks by having students use shoes or boots to
  - Order 3 or 4 shoes/boots from shortest to longest.
  - Use a balance scale to compare the mass of 2 different shoes/boots to determine which is heavier/lighter.
- As another extension, have students create boot glyphs to show personal information.

Decide on the glyph representations together with the class. For example:

- Boot colour: girl – red; boy – yellow
- Age: number of stripes on the boot top
- Favourite colour: colour of the boot's laces

Note: A glyph is a pictorial representation of data. A legend provides interpretation for the representations. For this problem, a template (included on page 66) is decorated to show the selected data.

Date: _____   Name: _____

Juan Counts Boots and Shoes

After recess, Juan looks at all the muddy boots and shoes in the hall.

He sees 5 pairs of boots and 3 pairs of shoes.

How many boots does Juan see?

How many shoes does he see?

Does he see more boots or more shoes?

Think

Talk

Solve

Share

15A

Name: _____

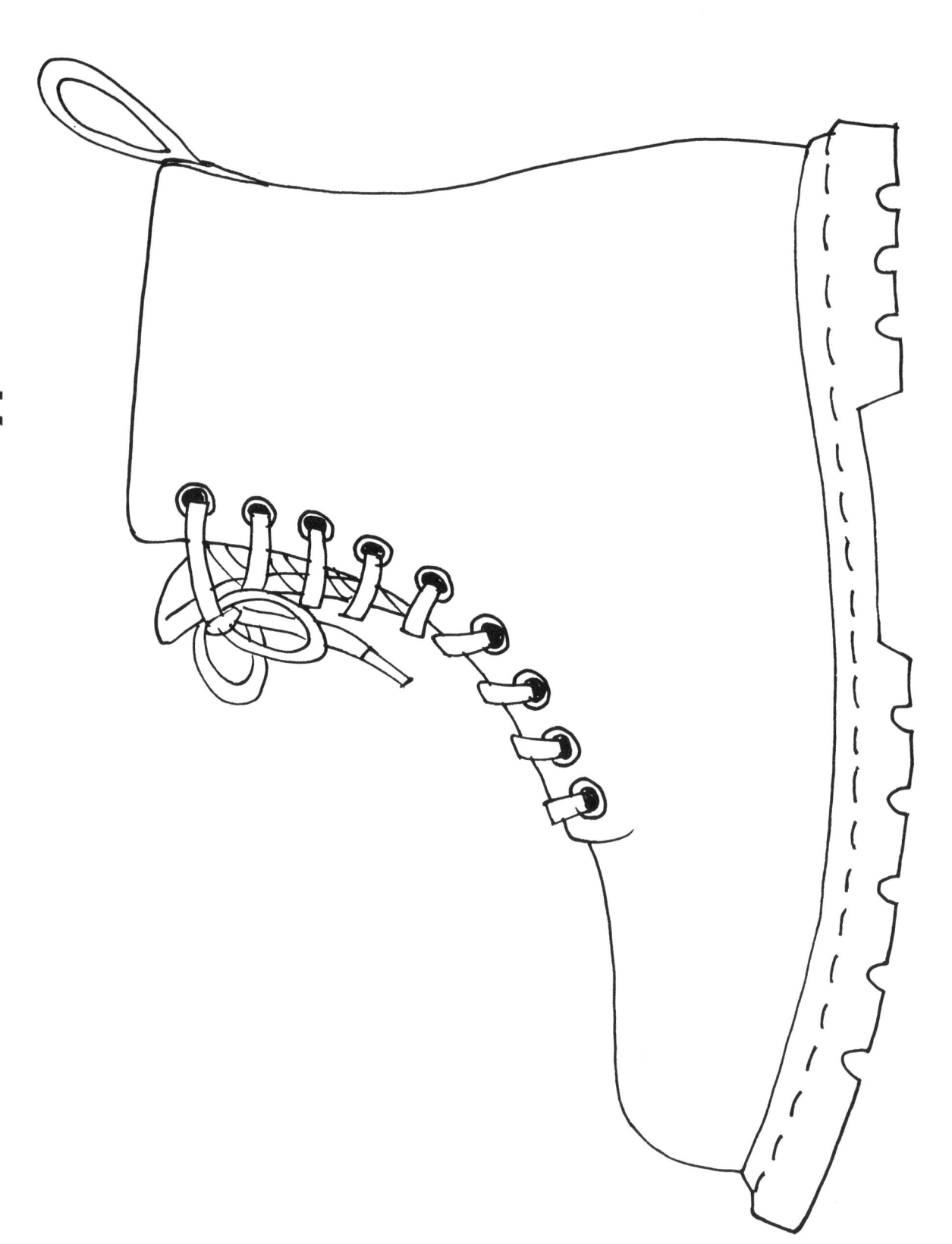

Date: _____

Boot Outline for Glyph

16A Pam Sees Ladybugs

Math Topic

Number

Math Concepts

- Counting by 5s
- Addition to 20
- Dot arrangements for 5
- Part-part-whole relationships

Problem Type

Addition: End result unknown (a + b = ?)

Problem

Pam sees 3 ladybugs on a plant.

Each ladybug has 5 spots.

How many spots are on all the ladybugs?

Background Information for Teachers

This problem focuses, in part, on concepts related to sets of 5. To scaffold this problem, consider the following activities:

- Practise counting by 5s using hands or dropping nickels into an empty can.
- Use five-frames for counting, as in the following example:

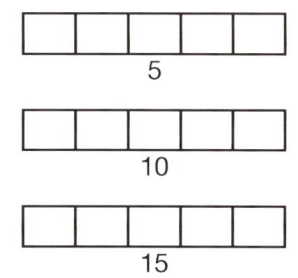

5

10

15

Students may use a variety of strategies to solve this problem, such as the following:

- Use manipulatives, such as hands or nickels.
- Draw circles for ladybugs and dots for spots, and count.
- Use empty five frames or ten frames with two-coloured counters, as in the following example.

- Use a number line with jumps to show skip counting.

Think

Talk

Solve

There are 15 spots altogether.

Share

Extend

- Cut out circular ladybug shapes from red construction paper. Draw a line to divide each ladybug in half. Discuss the fact that ladybugs have an equal number of spots on each half. Have students use counters to create various dot arrangements on their ladybugs. Discuss doubling as a means of determining the number of spots on the ladybug by counting the spots on one half and then doubling that number. As an added challenge, students can cover half of their ladybugs to provide a screened task, and then challenge classmates to determine the total number of spots on the ladybug.

Routine Problems

16A

- As another extension have students play "Ladybug Mingle." Help them make paper-plate ladybugs with 5 spots on each side (10 spots in total). Ask students to hold their ladybugs as they walk around the room. When you (or a student volunteer) call(s) out, "Mingle!" have students form groups of up to 10 students. Then, ask students to count the total number of ladybug spots in their group.

Note: Groups can be asked to count spots by 5s or 10s to reinforce these concepts.

Date: _____ Name: _____

Pam Sees Ladybugs

Pam sees 3 ladybugs on a plant.

Each ladybug has 5 spots.

How many spots are on all the ladybugs together?

Think

Talk

Solve

Share

16A

17A | Liam Plants Seeds

Math Topic
Number

Math Concepts
- Counting by 5s
- Counting on by 1s
- Addition to 20

Problem Type
Addition: End result unknown (a + b = ?)

Problem
Liam is planting seeds to make a greener world!

In one garden, Liam plants one row of 5 bean seeds, one row of 5 carrot seeds, and one row of 5 tomato seeds.

Liam has 3 bean seeds left over.

He adds 1 bean seed to each row.

How many seeds does Liam plant?

Background Information for Teachers
This problem is based on the book *The Curious Garden*, by Peter Brown, the story of a boy named Liam who tries to make a greener world by planting gardens throughout urban areas. To engage students, consider reading and discussing this book prior to posing the problem.

In order to approach this problem successfully, students will benefit from prior practice counting forward by 1s from any given number, and counting by 5s.

Students may use a variety of strategies to solve this problem, such as the following:

- Draw a picture of the garden.
- Count by 5s, and then count on by 1s.
- Use a number line to show skip counting.

Think
Talk
Solve
Liam plants 18 seeds.

Share
Assessment of Learning
Observe students as they solve this problem, or similar problems in the same number range, to determine which of the following strategies they are using:

- Use manipulatives to solve
- Draw pictures
- Count by 1s
- Skip count
- Count on
- Make groups
- Use their own strategies

Record observations on a copy of the Anecdotal Record sheet, found on page 16.

Extend
- Present the following extension problem to students:

  Eighteen plants grow from Liam's seeds.

  He pulls out all the carrots.

  How many plants are left growing in the garden?

- As another extension, have students draw their own gardens and use pictures, numbers, or words to describe it.

Date: _____   Name: _____

Liam Plants Seeds

Liam is planting seeds to make a greener world!

In one garden, Liam plants one row of 5 bean seeds, one row of 5 carrot seeds, and one row of 5 tomato seeds.

Liam has 3 bean seeds left over.

He adds 1 bean seed to each row.

How many seeds does Liam plant?

Think

Talk

Solve

Share

18A | Jacob Paints Pictures to Hang

Math Topic
Number

Math Concepts
- Addition to 20
- Counting by 2s
- Using equal groups to count sets

Problem Type
Addition: End result unknown (a + b = ?)

Problem
Jacob loves to paint pictures.

He paints 8 pictures to decorate his bedroom.

He hangs each picture with 2 tacks.

How many tacks does Jacob need to hang all 8 pictures?

Background information for Teachers

For this problem, students should be familiar with counting by 2s. To scaffold, use photographs of students to count feet or pictures of animals to count eyes.

Using visuals and concrete objects will reinforce counting by 2s as a more automatic response, as in rote counting.

Students may use a variety of strategies to solve this problem, such as the following:

- Draw a picture.
- Use manipulatives.
- Use a number line to skip count.

Think

Talk

Solve
Jacob needs 16 tacks.

Share

Extend

Have students brainstorm things that come in pairs, and record these on a chart. Then, have them use something from the chart create their own problems. This will reinforce the fact that the number of pairs is necessary to solve the problem by counting by 2s. These problems could be used to make a class book.

Jacob Paints Pictures to Hang

Jacob loves to paint pictures.

He paints 8 pictures to decorate his bedroom.

He hangs each picture with 2 tacks.

How many tacks does Jacob need to hang all 8 pictures?

Think

Talk

Solve

Share

19A | Pat Is Making Pumpkin Cookies

Math Topic
Number

Math Concepts
- Addition to 20
- Counting by 2s
- Counting on by 1s

Problem Type
Addition: End result unknown (a + b = ?)

Problem
Pat is making pumpkin cookies.

She uses 2 mint candies for the eyes, 1 jellybean candy for the nose, and 1 piece of licorice for the mouth.

She makes 5 cookies.

How many mints does Pat use for eyes for all the cookies?

How many jellybeans does she use for noses for all the cookies?

How many pieces of licorice does she use for mouths for all the cookies?

How many candies does Pat use altogether?

Background Information for Teachers

Students may use a variety of strategies to solve this problem, such as the following:

- Use math manipulatives, such as counters or interlocking cubes, to act out the problem.
- Draw a picture.
- Use a number line to skip count by 2s and then 1s, or by 4s and then 1s.

Think

Talk

Solve

Pat uses 10 mints for the eyes.

She uses 5 jellybeans for the noses.

She uses 5 pieces of licorice for mouths.

Pat uses 20 candies altogether to make the cookies.

Share

Extend

- Provide students with the following three extension problems:
    - How many eyes are there on 10 cookies?
    - If 1 long piece of licorice is cut into 3 pieces for 3 mouths, how many mouths do 2 long pieces of licorice make?
    - If each cookie costs 2 cents, how much would it cost to buy all 10 cookies?
- As an additional extension, have students use construction paper circles to make paper cookies, adding stickers for eyes, noses, and mouths. They can then use the cookies for counting activities, as well as for addition and doubling strategies.

Date: _____   Name: _____

Pat Is Making Pumpkin Cookies

Pat is making pumpkin cookies.

She uses 2 mint candies for the eyes, 1 jellybean candy for the nose, and 1 piece of licorice for the mouth.

She makes 5 cookies.

How many mints does Pat use for eyes for all the cookies?

How many jellybeans does she use for noses for all the cookies?

How many pieces of licorice does she use for mouths for all the cookies?

How many candies does Pat use altogether?

Think

Talk

Solve

Share

19A

20A | Tariq and the Horses

Math Topic
Number

Math Concepts
- Subtraction to 20
- Comparing sets

Problem Type
Subtraction: End result unknown (a – b = ?)

Problem
Tariq lives on a farm.

They have 14 horses.

He opens the barn doors and lets out 8 horses.

How many horses are left inside the barn?

Background Information for Teachers
Students' understanding of the relationship between addition and subtraction using the part-part-whole concept will help them to understand this problem.

Students may use a variety of strategies to solve this problem, such as the following:

- Draw a picture.
- Use a number line, and make jumps of 1, beginning at 8 to 14.
- Use math manipulatives to act out the problem.
- Use an equation: 14 – 8 = ?

Think

Talk

Solve
There are 6 horses left inside the barn.

Share

Extend
Have students use concrete materials to explore the part-part-whole relationship for the number 14. Provide each student with 14 two-sided counters. Ask them to use the counters to create two sets, and record the equation on chart paper or the white board (for example, 9 + 5 = 14). Have students complete the fact family for this equation. Encourage students to find as many different sets as possible for 14.

Assessment as Learning
Have students complete a Problem-Solving Journal page to reflect on their experience with the extension activity above. Encourage students to share their learning through pictures, numbers, and words, focusing on what they did in the task, what they learned, and about what they would like to learn more.

Date: _____ Name: _____

Tariq and the Horses

Tariq lives on a farm.

They have 14 horses.

He opens the barn doors and lets out 8 horses.

How many horses are left inside the barn?

Think

Talk

Solve

Share

21A | Janet's Birthday Party

Math Topic

Number

Math Concept

Addition

Problem Type

Addition: End result unknown (a + b = ?)

Problem

Janet is having a birthday party.

Janet is 3 years older than her sister, Katie.

Katie is 9 years old and had 9 candles on her cake.

How many candles are on Janet's cake?

Background Information for Teachers

Although students will be familiar with addition problems by this point, this problem presents a different format. It is not a problem for which students can use subtraction to find the solution. This might present a challenge for them to choose strategies for solving the problem.

Students may use a variety of strategies to solve this problem, such as the following:

- Draw a picture, and count on, or count back.
- Use manipulatives to act out the problem (provide sticks or actual candles instead of counters or cubes).
- Use a number line to count on.
- Use a beaded frame card.
- Write an equation: 9 + 3 = ?

Think

Talk

Solve

There are 12 candles on Janet's cake.

Share

Extend

- Provide students with this extension problem:

    Janet has orange and white candles on her cake.

    She has an equal number of each colour of candle.

    How many candles does she have in each colour?

    Differentiate this problem by increasing or decreasing the number of candles on the cake. This problem helps with students' developmental math skills and concepts related to doubling, halving, and equal sets.

- As an added exploration of part-part-whole relationships and comparison of sets, ask:

    What if there is not an equal number of white and orange candles? What are all the possible combinations of 12 candles?

    Have students draw the cakes and candles.

Date: _____   Name: _____

Janet's Birthday Party

Janet is having a birthday party.

Janet is 3 years older than her sister, Katie.

Katie is 9 years old and had 9 candles on her cake.

How many candles are on Janet's cake?

Think

Talk

Solve

Share

21A

22A | Mrs. Joyal's Class Goes Swimming

Math Topic

Number

Math Concept

Addition

Problem Type

Addition: End result unknown (a + b = ?)

Problem

Mrs. Joyal's class is going swimming.

There are more girls in the class than there are boys.

There are _____ girls in the pool.

There are _____ boys in the pool.

Altogether there are _____ of Mrs. Joyal's students in the pool.

Use all three of the numbers below, in the correct places, to complete the problem:

      11   20   9

Background Information for Teachers

This addition story will help students

- Read and interpret an addition problem
- Use number sense to decide where each of the numbers belongs
- Justify their decision(s).

Students may use a variety of strategies to solve this problem, such as the following:

- Use number tiles or squares of paper with numerals recorded on them to manipulate the numbers in the problem, as in the following example.

    | 11 | | 9 | | 20 |

- Use manipulatives to act out the problem.

Think

Talk

Solve

There are 11 girls in the pool.

There are 9 boys in the pool.

Altogether there are 20 children in the pool.

Share

Extend

- Present the following extension problem to students:

    How many more girls are there than boys in the pool?

    Have students use a comparison model to explore this problem. Provide them with two-sided counters. Have each student create one set of 11 counters to represent the girls and line up the set of 9 boys underneath to visually show comparison.

    ●●●●●●●●●●●
    ○○○○○○○○○

    Students can then clearly see, compare, and count the difference.

- To extend this problem even further to an open-ended challenge, ask students:

    Mr. Beto's grade 1 class also goes swimming.

    There are 20 students in the class.

    Some are boys and some are girls.

    How many of each might there be?

    Provide students with double ten-frames (included in the Appendix on page 245) and two-sided counters, and have them find

▶

80   Hands-On Problem Solving • Grade 1

22A

possible combinations to record as fact families, such as

5 + 15 = 20

15 + 5 = 20

20 − 5 = 15

20 − 15 = 5

Routine Problems

Date: _____   Name: _____

Mrs. Joyal's Class Goes Swimming

Mrs. Joyal's class is going swimming.

There are more girls in the class than there are boys.

There are _____ girls in the pool.

There are _____ boys in the pool.

Altogether there are _____ of Mrs. Joyal's students in the pool.

Use all three numbers below, in the correct places, to complete the problem:

        11   20   9.

Think

Talk

Solve

Share

23A | Hot Chocolate for the School Patrols

Math Topic

Number

Math Concepts

- Skip counting by 5s
- Counting sets
- Addition

Problem Type

Addition: End result unknown (a + b = ?)

Problem

On winter days, our teacher makes a cup of hot chocolate for each of the school patrols.

There are 6 patrols.

Our teacher puts 5 marshmallows into each cup.

How many marshmallows does he use on one winter day?

Background Information for Teachers

This problem involves counting by 5s and, by this point, students have begun developing a bank of strategies for solving such problems. As a result, there is a progressive hierarchy of ways that students might count the marshmallows:

- 1, 2, 3…30
- 5, 10, 11, 12, 13…30
- 5, 10, 15, 16, 17, 18…30
- 5, 10, 15, 20…30
- 10, 20, 30

Students may use a variety of strategies to solve this problem, such as the following:

- Draw a picture of 6 cups with 5 marshmallows in each, and count by 5s.
- Use manipulatives to act out the problem by making 6 sets of 5.

- Record tallies as in the following example.

  ||||| ||||| ||||| ||||| ||||| |||||

- Use a hundred chart (included in the Appendix on page 246) to count by 5s.

Think

Talk

Solve

Our teacher uses 30 marshmallows for hot chocolate on one winter day.

Share

Extend

- Have students colour in squares on a hundred chart (included in the Appendix on page 246) for counting by 5s. Give students several opportunities to do this (using several hundred charts each), starting at different points, to observe that the type of pattern is consistent.

- As an additional extension, pose the following problem to students:

  On a snowy day, our class has toboggan races on the school hill.

  My friend, Max, goes down the hill in 5 seconds.

  My other friend, Avery, goes down the hill in 10 seconds.

  I go down the hill in 7 seconds.

  How close is my time to each of my friends' times?

Note: This problem allows students an opportunity to focus on relating anchors to 5 and 10 (7 is 2 more than 5 and 3 less than 10).

Routine Problems

Date: _____   Name: _____

Hot Chocolate for the School Patrols

On winter days, our teacher makes a cup of hot chocolate for each of the school patrols.

There are 6 patrols.

Our teacher puts 5 marshmallows into each cup.

How many marshmallows does he use on one winter day?

Think

Talk

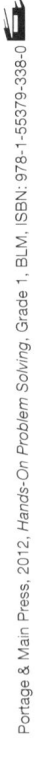

Solve

Share

24A | People on the Bus

Math Topic

Number

Math Concepts

- Subtraction
- Addition

Problem Type

- Addition: End result unknown (a + b = ?)
- Subtraction: End result unknown (a − b = ?)

Problem

There are 16 people on the bus.

3 people get off the bus, and 5 more get on.

How many people are on the bus now?

Background Information for Teachers

This problem involves both addition and subtraction. Modeling this problem type will allow students to be more successful with it. To scaffold the problem, present the following scenarios, and model them on a number line:

- I have 10 pencils.
  I use up 5 of them at school.
  I get 2 more from home.
  How many pencils do I have now?

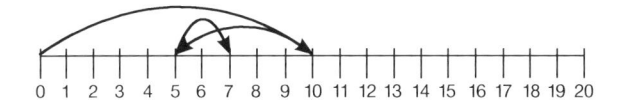

- Joey has 8 cherries.
  He picks 3 more from the tree.
  He eats 5 cherries.
  How many are left?

Students may use a variety of strategies to solve this problem, such as the following:

- Draw a picture to represent the 16 people, and count on and back.
- Use math manipulatives to act out the problem.
- Use a number line to count on and count back.
- Use a beaded frame card with 2 rows of 10 beads.

Think

Talk

Solve

There are 18 people on the bus now.

Share

Extend

Have students work in pairs to play the "Bus Game". Provide each student with 14 interlocking cubes and a number cube (die). Have each student use all 14 cubes, arranged in 2s, to create a "bus", as in the following example:

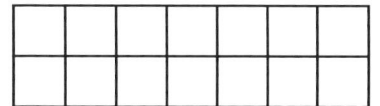

Have player A from each pair roll a die and subtract that number from 14, removing the appropriate number of cubes from his or her bus. Then, have player B from each pair roll a die, subtract that number from 14, and remove the appropriate number of cubes from his or her bus. Next, have player A roll the die again, this time *adding on* the number of cubes rolled to his or her bus. Ask player B to do the same. Have play continue, with partners taking turns

▶

Routine Problems

24A

rolling the die, until each player has subtracted cubes twice from his or her bus and added cubes twice. Then, ask the players to compare their buses to determine whose is longer—which student in the pair has the bus with more cubes.

People on the Bus

There are 16 people on the bus.

3 people got off the bus, and 5 more got on.

How many people are on the bus now?

Think

Talk

Solve

Share

25A | Janey Plants Corn, Beans, and Squash

Math Topic

Number

Math Concepts

- Counting sets
- Addition

Problem Type

Addition: End result unknown (a + b = ?)

Problem

Corn, beans, and squash grow well together.

Janey digs 6 holes in her garden.

She plans to put one of each type of plant into each hole.

How many plants does Janey need?

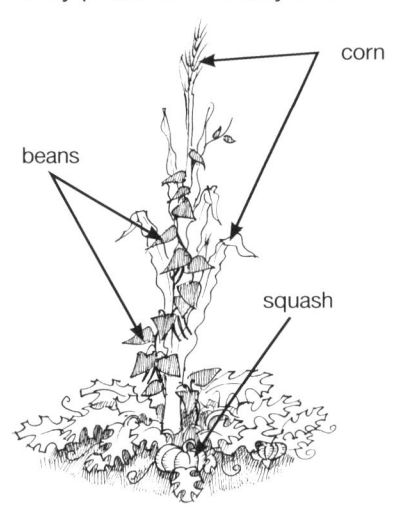

Background Information for Teachers

The Three Sisters are the three main crops of various First Nations people, and are often planted together. The beans climb up the corn plants for support, so they do not need poles, and they nourish the soil. The squash blocks the sun and stops weeds from growing.

This type of problem provides teachers with information about students' levels of understanding, based on the strategies they use to solve it. For example, if students always rely on manipulatives, they should be provided with opportunities to explore other strategies.

Students may use a variety of strategies to solve this problem, such as the following:

- Draw a picture of the 6 holes and the 3 plants in each hole.
- Use manipulatives to act out the problem by making 6 sets of 3.
- Use a number line to make 6 jumps of 3.

Think

Talk

Solve

Janey needs 18 plants.

Share

Extend

Present this extension problem to students:

After Janey harvests her crop, she uses the vegetables to make chili.

Janey invites 4 of her friends for chili night.

On a table, she puts out a cup, a spoon, a bowl, and a plate for each person.

How many things does Janey put on the table?

Don't forget about Janey!

Date: _____   Name: _____

Janey Plants Corn, Beans, and Squash

Corn, beans, and squash grow well together.

Janey digs 6 holes in her garden.

She plans to put one of each type of plant into each hole.

How many plants does Janey need?

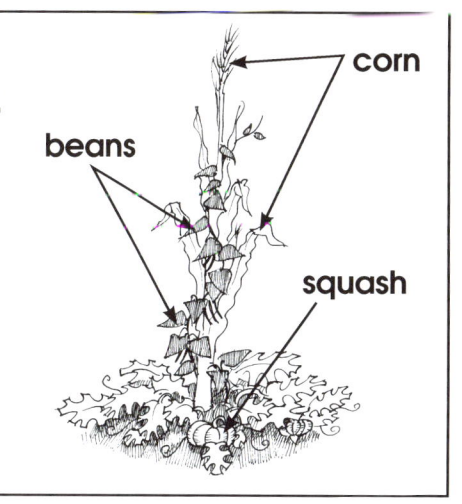

corn
beans
squash

Think

Talk

Solve

Share

25A

26A | Ricardo Puts Money Into his Piggy Bank

Math Topic
Number

Math Concept
Counting by 10s

Problem Type
Addition: End result unknown (a + b = ?)

Problem
Ricardo puts 10 cents into his piggy bank every Tuesday and Friday.

How much money does Ricardo have after 4 weeks?

Background Information for Teachers
For this problem, students will benefit from reviewing counting by 10s, as well as the days of the week.

Students may use a variety of strategies to solve this problem, such as the following:

- Draw a picture of coins with 10 cents marked on them, and count by 10s.
- Use plastic coins to dramatize the problem.
- Count by 10s: 10, 20, 30, 40, 50, 60, 70, 80.
- Use a hundred chart to count by 10s.
- Use a classroom calendar to mark each. Tuesday and Friday, and place play money (dimes) on the calendar.

Think

Talk

Solve
Ricardo has 80 cents in the bank after 4 weeks.

Share

Extend
Provide students with the following extension problem:

For how many more days does Ricardo need to put 10 cents into his bank to make 1 dollar?

Date: _____   Name: _____

Ricardo Puts Money Into his Piggy Bank

Ricardo puts 10 cents into his piggy bank every Tuesday and Friday.

How much money does Ricardo have after 4 weeks?

Think

Talk

Solve

Share

27A | Gobin Sees Bugs in the Garden

Math Topic

Number

Math Concept

Addition

Problem Type

Addition: End result unknown (a + b = ?)

Problem

Gobin sees some bugs in the garden.

He sees a ladybug and a spider.

How many legs does Gobin see on the bugs?

Background Information for Teachers

This problem connects well to science and the study of animals. To do the problem, students will need to know how many legs each bug has. Before presenting the problem, display photographs of insects and spiders for students to observe and discuss.

Students may use a variety of strategies to solve this problem, such as the following:

- Draw a picture of each bug, and count the legs.
- Use a number line to count on.
- Write an equation: 6 + 8 = ?

Think

Talk

Solve

Gobin sees 14 legs on the bugs.

Share

Extend

- Provide students with this extension problem:

    Are there more legs on 3 ladybugs or 2 spiders?

    How many more?

- As an additional extension, have students use cream-filled cookies and pieces of shoelace licorice to make bug cookies as in the following illustration:

    Have students create both insects and arachnids and then explore combinations and comparisons.

Date: _____ Name: _____

Gobin Sees Bugs in the Garden

Gobin sees some bugs in the garden.

He sees a ladybug and a spider.

How many legs does Gobin see on the bugs?

Think

Talk

Solve

Share

27A

28A | A Seesaw at Brownlee School

Math Topic
Variables and Equations

Math Concept
Equality

Problem
Brownlee School has a new playground.

There is a 4-seat sea saw.

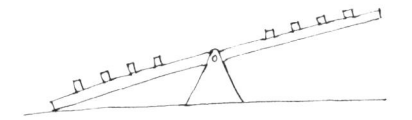

Draw a picture of students on the sea saw when it is balanced and when it is not balanced.

Use numbers and words to describe your picture.

Background Information for Teachers

To solve this problem successfully, students will benefit from previous exposure to the concept of equality and inequality. Before posing this problem to students consider engaging them in the assessment-for-learning task below.

Students may use a variety of strategies to solve this problem, such as the following:

- Use balance scales to determine equality and inequality.
- Draw pictures, and compare sets.

Assessment for Learning

To assess their understanding of equality and inequality, have students work with pan scales and interlocking cubes to determine equality by balancing the scales. For example:

- Place 5 cubes on one pan. How many cubes do you need to put on the other pan to balance the scale?

- Place 6 cubes on one pan and 4 cubes on the other. Are the sets equal? How can you make them equal?

Use copies of the Anecdotal record sheet, included on page 16, to record your results.

Think

Talk

Solve

Note: Students' pictures and answers may vary.

To balance the sea saw, there must be an equal number of students on each side.

Balanced

Unbalanced

Share

Extend

Present the following extension problem to students:

There are 4 children on each side of the sea saw. How many shoes are they wearing altogether?

94   Hands-On Problem Solving • Grade 1

Date: _____   Name: _____

A Seesaw at Brownlee School

Brownlee School has a new playground.

There is a 4-seat seasaw.

Draw a picture of students on the seasaw when it is balanced and when it is not balanced.

Use numbers and words to describe your picture.

Think

Talk

Solve

Share

28A

29A | Emma Takes Gymnastics Lessons

Math Topics
- Patterns
- Number

Math Concepts
- Repeating patterns
- Doubles

Problem Type
Addition: End result unknown (a + b = ?)

Problem
Emma takes gymnastics lessons on Wednesdays and Saturdays.

Each lesson is 2 hours long.

How many hours of gymnastics does Emma take each week?

How many hours of gymnastics does Emma take in 2 weeks?

Background Information for Teachers
Prior to presenting this problem to students, review the days of the week and repeating events on the class calendar. For example

- How many music classes do we have this week?
- How many gym classes do we have this week?
- How many lunch hours do we have this week?

Students may use a variety of strategies to solve this problem, such as the following:

- Use a classroom calendar and counters or cubes to represent hours of gymnastics.
- Count by 2s.
- Write an equation:
  2 + 2 = 4; 2 + 2 + 2 + 2 = 8.
- Use doubles: 2 + 2 = 4 , 4 + 4 = 8.

Students should have access to math materials at all times to allow them to implement a chosen strategy.

Think

Talk

Solve
Emma takes gymnastics for 4 hours in 1 week and for 8 hours in 2 weeks.

Share

Extend
- Provide students with the following extension problem:

  Record how much you read at home. Give yourself a checkmark for each page you read. After two weeks, circle groups of ten checkmarks to see how many pages you read.

- As an alternate extension, have students record their favourite extracurricular activities and then use a calendar or tally chart to record how often they participate in this activity over a two-week period. Have students report back to the class.

Date: _____   Name: _____

Emma Takes Gymnastics Lessons

Emma takes gymnastics lessons on Wednesdays and Saturdays.

Each lesson is 2 hours long.

How many hours of gymnastics does Emma take each week?

How many hours of gymnastics does Emma take in 2 weeks?

Think

Talk

Solve

Share

29A

30A | Ming Makes a Pattern With Lights

Math Topic

Patterns

Math Concept

Repeating pattern

Problem

Ming buys orange, yellow, and green lights to decorate her garden.

She begins a pattern with the lights: *green, orange, yellow, yellow.*

If she repeats the pattern 3 more times, how many lights of each colour does Ming need?

How many lights does she use altogether?

Background Information for Teachers

In order to explore and solve problems that involve patterns, students should have access to manipulatives, such as interlocking cubes and coloured counters. Consider spray painting lima beans in the three colours referred to in the problem, and use these for other activities throughout the year.

Students may use a variety of strategies to solve this problem, such as the following:

- Use manipulatives, such as interlocking cubes or coloured counters.
- Draw a picture of the pattern.

Think

Talk

Solve

Ming uses 4 green lights, 4 orange lights, and 8 yellow lights.

She uses 16 lights altogether.

Share

Extend

Have students name the pattern (*ABCC*) and then use actions or sounds to translate it another way. For example:

- *slap clap stomp stomp*

Date: _____   Name: _____

Ming Makes a Pattern With Lights

Ming buys orange, yellow, and green lights to decorate her garden.

She begins a pattern with the lights: *green, orange, yellow, yellow*.

If she repeats the pattern 3 more times, how many lights of each colour does Ming need?

How many lights does she use altogether?

Think

Talk

Solve

Share

30A

31A | Tina Is Making a Bracelet

Math Topic

Patterns

Math Concept

Repeating patterns

Problem

Tina is making a bracelet.

She makes this bead pattern: *blue, yellow, white, blue, yellow, white, blue, yellow, white…*

If this pattern continues, what colour will the 10th bead be?

How do you know?

Background Information for Teachers

For this problem, students should have experience identifying the core of a pattern, and extending the pattern to determine the bead colour.

Students may use various strategies to solve this problem, such as the following:

- Use cubes to reproduce the pattern.
- Draw the pattern of coloured beads.

Think

Talk

Solve

The tenth bead is blue, because the pattern goes *blue yellow white*. The 9th bead is white, so the 10th bead is blue.

Share

Extend

- Provide students with this extension problem:

    Use coloured beads to create an *AABB* pattern for a beaded belt. What colour will the 12th bead be? How do you know?

- As an additional extension, have students use actions to create an *AABB* pattern. For example: *jump, squat, blink, squat*.

Date: _____   Name: _____

Tina Is Making a Bracelet

Tina is making a bracelet.

She makes this bead pattern: *blue, yellow, white, blue, yellow, white, blue, yellow, white...*

If this pattern continues, what colour will the 10th bead be?

How do you know?

Think

Talk

Solve

Share

32A | Jeremy Makes a Pattern

Math Topic

Patterns

Math Concept

Repeating patterns

Problem

Jeremy is playing with his toy cars, trucks, and buses.

He lines them up in a pattern like this:

Which toy goes in the empty space?

What is the 15th toy in the pattern?

Background Information for Teachers

Students may use a variety of strategies to solve this problem, such as the following:

- Use manipulatives, such as toy vehicles, to complete the pattern.
- Draw the pattern.
- Identify the pattern core, and use it to extend the pattern.

Think

Talk

Solve

A truck goes in the empty space.

The 15th toy is a truck.

Share

Extend

Have students use pictures from toy flyers or automobile dealerships to represent the pattern.

Jeremy Makes a Pattern

Jeremy is playing with his toy cars, trucks, and buses.

He lines them up in a pattern like this:

Which toy goes in the empty space?

What is the 15th toy in the pattern?

Think

Talk

Solve

Share

33A | Barry and Devon Help Build Patios

Math Topic
Measurement

Math Concept
Comparing area

Problem

Both Barry and Devon are helping their families build backyard patios.

The plan is to cover each patio with square blocks.

Each boy draws the shape of his patio, as shown:

Devon's Deck

Barry's Deck

Which patio needs more blocks?

How do you know?

Note: The student activity sheet for this problem is spread out over two pages.

Background Information for Teachers

Understanding surface area can be an abstract concept for young students. It is therefore important to approach such tasks using hands-on materials to cover surfaces. For example, use blocks or cubes to cover shapes, and then count and compare the number of cubes used to cover each shape.

Students may use a variety of strategies to solve this problem, such as the following:

- Use manipulatives.

Note: Use a non-standard unit to cover and measure shapes, such as interlocking cubes or blocks.

Think

Talk

Solve

Devon needs more blocks for his patio.

We know, because we can count the number of blocks used to cover each deck and compare the sets.

Share

Extend

- Present the following extension problem to students:

  Draw two patios. Each patio should have a different shape, but both need exactly 16 blocks to cover it.

- As an added extension, have students use interlocking cubes to cover and compare various mystery shapes (included on pages 107–108).

Date: _____   Name: _____

Barry and Devon Help Build Patios

Both Barry and Devon are helping their families build backyard patios.

The plan is to cover each patio with square blocks.

Each boy draws the shape of his patio, as shown:

| Devon's Deck | Barry's Deck |

Which patio needs more blocks?

How do you know?

Barry and Devon Help Build Patios – Continued

Think

Talk

Solve

Share

Date: _____   Name: _____

Mystery Shapes

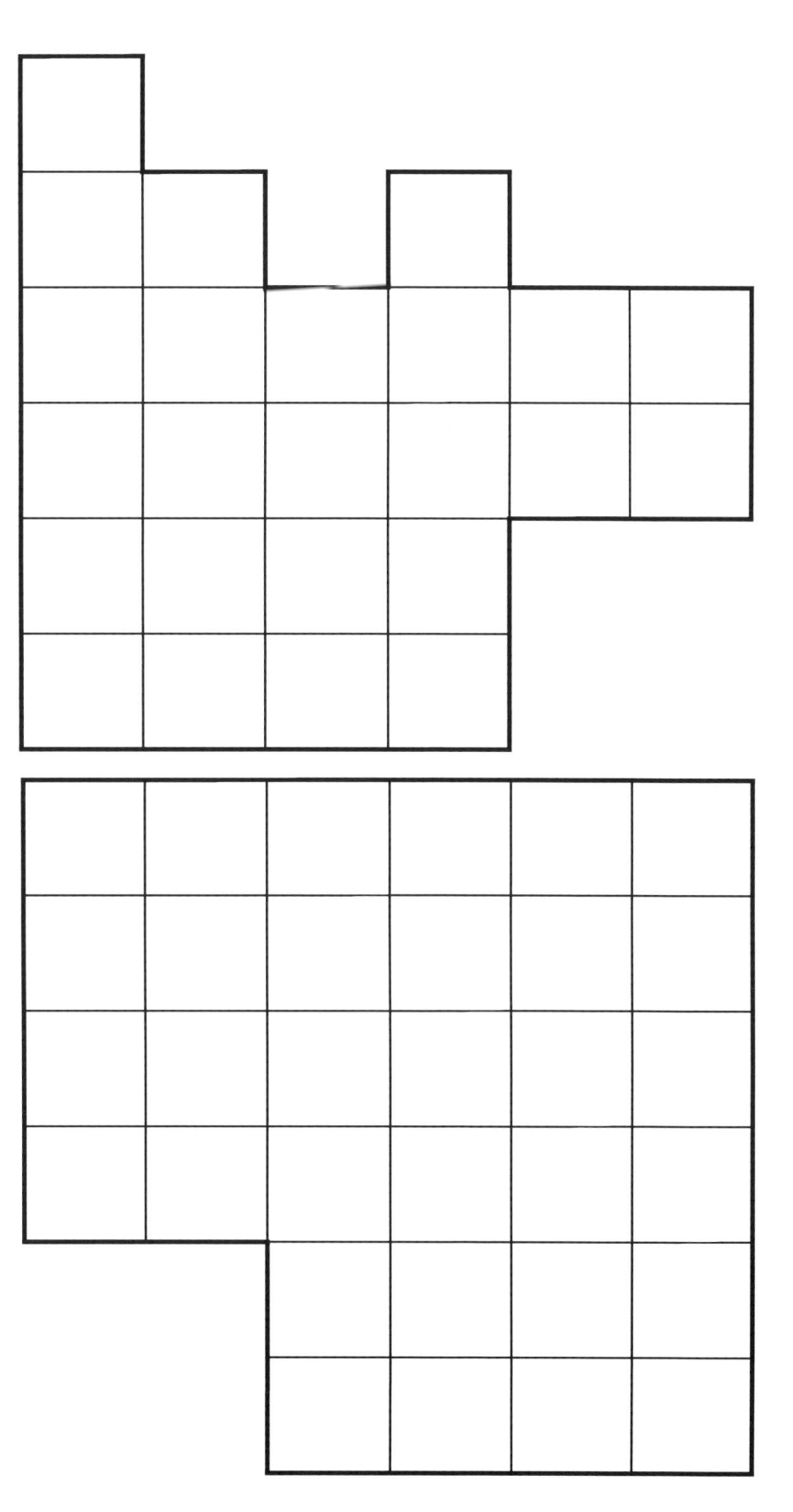

33A

Date: _____   Name: _____

Mystery Shapes – Continued

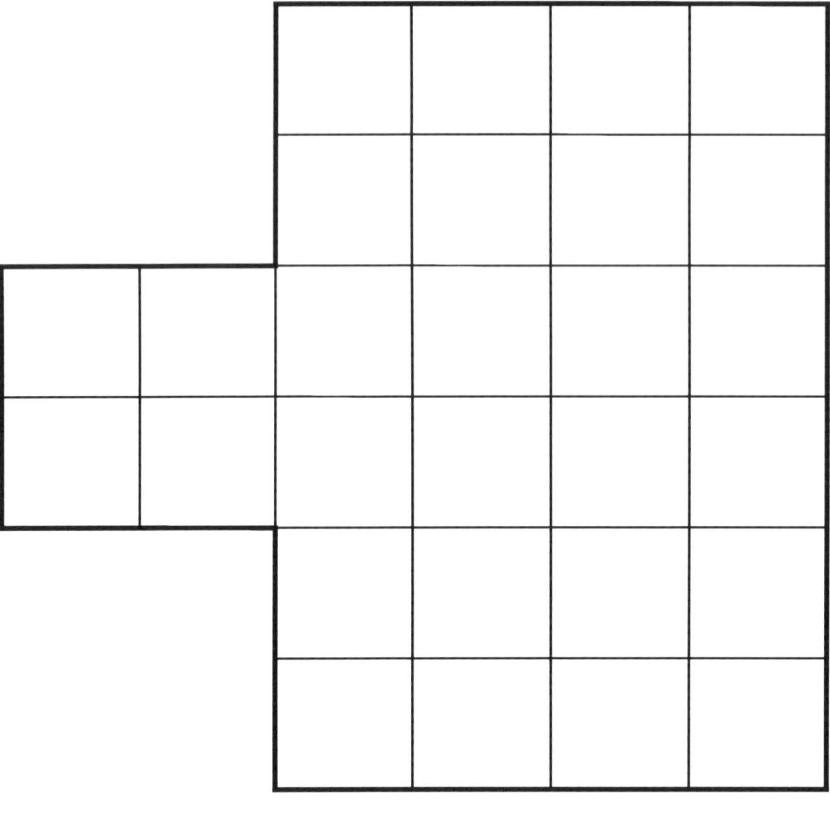

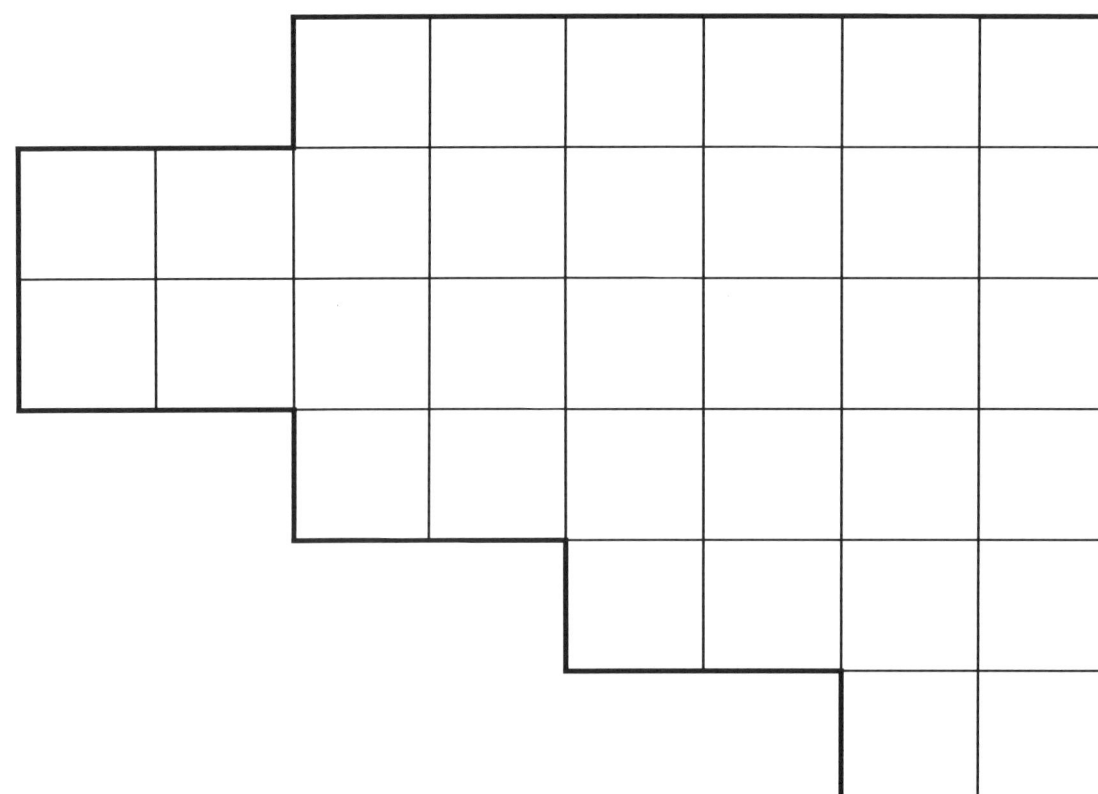

33A

34A | Max Draws Monkeys

Math Topic

Measurement

Math Concepts

- Comparing length
- Ordering by length

Problem

Max loves to draw monkeys.

He draws 4 monkeys with tails of different length.

Order the monkeys from the one with the longest tail to the one with the shortest tail.

Print their names in order.

Mimi   Manny   Moe   Mavis

Background Information for Teachers

In order to approach this problem, students should have experience using matching to compare objects by length.

Students may use a variety of strategies to solve this problem, such as the following:

- Use a piece of string or wool to compare tail lengths.
- Cut out the monkeys, and compare tail lengths.
- Use visual comparison.

Think

Talk

Solve

Longest tail ⟶ Shortest tail

Manny   Mavis   Mimi   Moe

Share

Extend

- Present these two extension problems to students:
    - How many eyes are on all 4 monkeys?
    - How many paws are on all 4 monkeys?

- As an additional extension, have students look through magazines for pictures of objects that can be measured and compared according to length. For example, find 3 or more pictures of cars, trees, houses, people, or animals, and order them from shortest to tallest or shortest to longest. Students can also use technology to find images that can be "stretched" and printed in different lengths.

Routine Problems

Date: _____   Name: _____

Max Draws Monkeys

Max loves to draw monkeys.

He draws 4 monkeys with tails of different length:

Mimi   Manny    Moe    Mavis

Order the monkeys from the one with the longest tail to the one with the shortest tail.

Print their names in order.

Think

Talk

Solve

Share

34A

35A | Carson Measures Objects on a Scale

Math Topic

Measurement

Math Concept

Comparing mass

Problem

Carson is measuring objects at a centre.

He puts two objects on a scale to see how heavy each one is.

Circle the heavier object on each scale.

Background Information for Teachers

In order to approach this problem with confidence, students will benefit from previous exposure to balance scales.

Students may use a variety of strategies to solve this problem, such as the following:

- Explore how a balance scale indicates heaviness of an object.
- Find similar objects in the classroom to measure on a balance scale.
- Use visual comparison.

Think

Talk

Solve

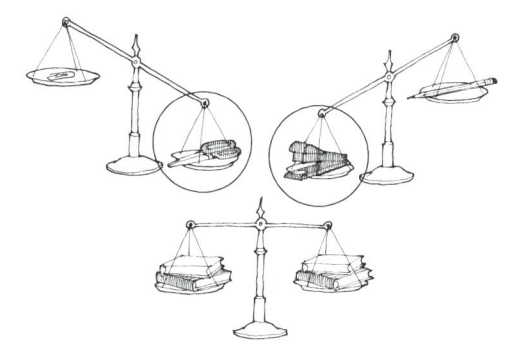

Share

Extend

Have students build objects out of clay, Plasticine, or play dough. Then, have them use a balance scale to compare the heaviness of their objects. Challenge students to make two objects that balance the scale.

Routine Problems

111

Date: _____   Name: _____

Carson Measures Objects on a Scale

Carson is measuring objects at a centre.

He puts two objects on a scale to see how heavy each one is.

Circle the heavier object on each scale.

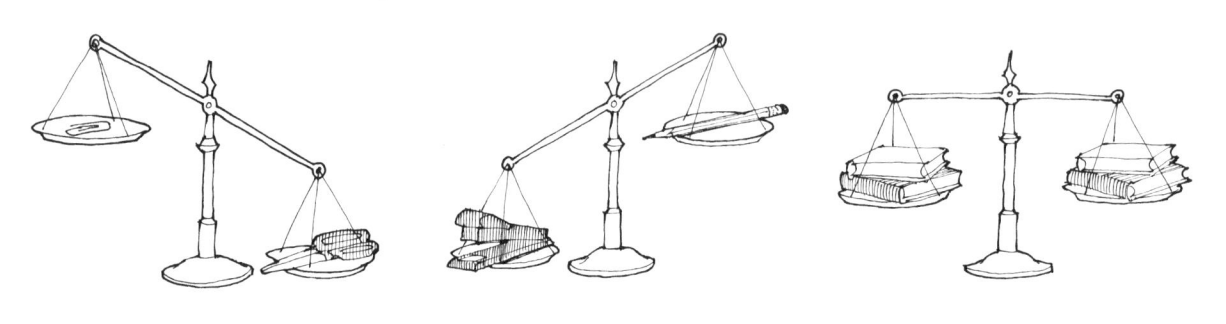

Think

Talk

Solve

Share

112

35A

36A | Manuel Sorts Shapes

Math Topic
Geometry

Math Concepts
- Comparing 2-D shapes
- Sorting 2-D shapes

Problem

Manuel is sorting shapes.

He has these shapes:

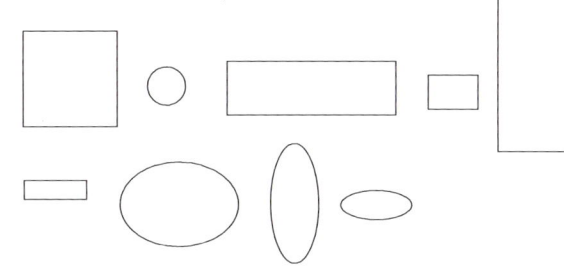

Sort the shapes into 2 groups.

How can you sort the shapes?

Background Information for Teachers

To solve this problem students need to be familiar with the mathematical language of two-dimensional shapes. A review of the terminology might be necessary before working on this problem with students.

Have students cut out the shapes on the two-dimensional shapes template (included in the Appendix on page 247) and use them for sorting.

Students may use a variety of strategies to solve this problem, such as the following:

- Use manipulatives (geoshapes) to act out the problem.
- Draw a picture of the sorted shapes.

Think

Talk

Solve

Students may find different ways to sort the shapes. For example:

- Shapes with 4 sides in one group, round and oval shapes in another group
- Small shapes in one group, larger shapes in another group
- Students may even colour the shapes and sort according to colour.

Share

Extend

Provide students with a collection of pattern blocks or geoblocks. Have them find blocks that do not fit into either of their two groups according so their sorting rule from the preceding problem. Encourage them to explain why the blocks do not fit according to their sorting rule.

Assessment of Learning

Observe students as they conduct the preceding extension activity, conferencing with them individually. Have students identify two blocks that do not fit into either of their sorting groups and explain why they do not fit the sorting rule.

Use the Individual Student Observations sheet, found on page 17, to record results.

Routine Problems

Date: _____   Name: _____

Manuel Sorts Shapes

Manuel is sorting shapes.

He has these shapes:

Sort the shapes into 2 groups.

How can you sort the shapes?

Think

Talk

Solve

Share

36A

37A | Sherry Plays With Pattern Blocks

Math Topics
- Geometry
- Number

Math Concepts
- Comparing 2-D shapes
- Counting
- Addition

Problem

Sherry is playing with pattern blocks.

She chooses these shapes to play with:

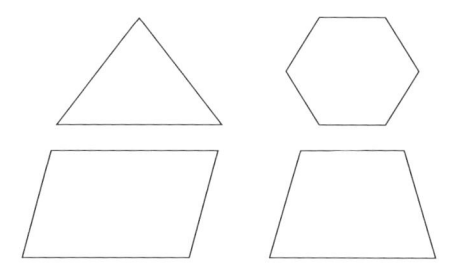

How many sides are there on all 4 shapes?

Background Information for Teachers

Students may use a variety of strategies to solve this problem, such as the following:

- Use manipulatives, such as pattern blocks, and count the sides.
- Use a number line to count on.
- Use a number sentence: 3 + 6 + 4 + 4 = ?

Think

Talk

Solve

There are 17 sides on the 4 shapes.

Share

Extend

Have students work with pattern blocks to find:

- 2 shapes that have 6 sides altogether.
- 2 shapes that have 7 sides altogether.
- 2 shapes that have 8 sides altogether.
- 4 shapes that have 14 sides altogether.

Have students record their work by tracing the shapes and including equations.

Routine Problems

Date: _____   Name: _____

Sherry Plays With Pattern Blocks

Sherry is playing with pattern blocks.

She chooses these shapes to play with:

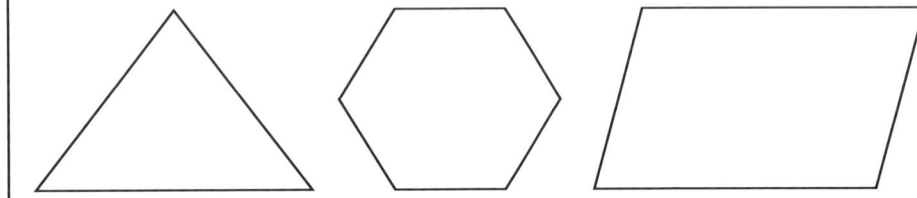

How many sides are there on all 4 shapes?

Think

Talk

Solve

Share

37A

38A | Steven makes Patterns With Shape Stickers

Math Topics
- Geometry
- Patterns

Math Concept
Two-dimensional shapes

Problem
Steven is making patterns with shape stickers.

He has triangles, circles, and squares.

He repeats a pattern 3 times.

What might Steven's pattern look like?

Use the shapes to make the pattern.

Background Information for Teachers
To solve this problem, students will require an understanding of the characteristics of 2-D shapes. They will also benefit from previous exposure to creating and translating patterns. To scaffold this problem, provide students with pattern blocks, and have them create patterns with specified cores, such as.

- *ABC*
- *clap, clap, snap*

Have students use the shapes templates (included in the Appendix on page 247) to explore patterns with 2-D shapes.

Students may use a variety of strategies to solve this problem, such as the following:

- Use manipulatives (geoshapes) to act out the problem.
- Draw a picture of the pattern.

Think

Talk

Solve
There are various solutions possible, including

ABC:

△○□ △○□ △○□

ABAC:

△○△□ △○△□ △○△□

AABBCC:

△△○○□□ △△○○□□ △△○○□□

Share

Extend
- Provide students with the following extension problem:

    How many circles, squares, and triangles are in the pattern you made for Steven?

Note: To solve this problem, students should refer back to the pattern they created in the main problem for this lesson-plan.

Routine Problems

Date: _____   Name: _____

Steven makes Patterns With Shape Stickers

Steven is making patterns with shape stickers.

He has triangles, circles, and squares.

He repeats a pattern 3 times.

What might Steven's pattern look like?

Use the shapes to make the pattern.

Think

Talk

Solve

Share

39A | Aiden Sorts Three-Dimensional Objects

Math Topic
Geometry

Math Concepts
- Comparing three-dimensional objects
- Sorting three-dimensional objects

Problem
Aiden is sorting three-dimensional (3-D) objects:

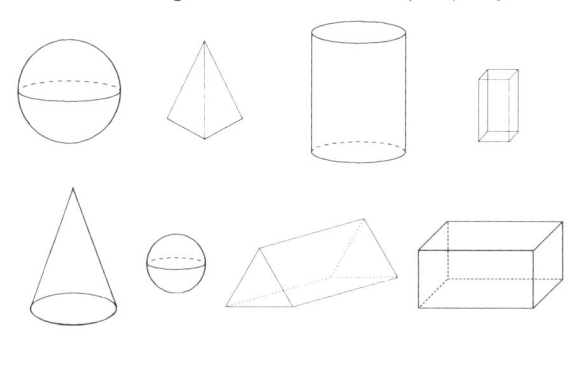

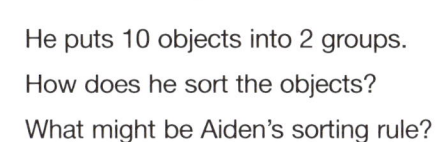

He puts 10 objects into 2 groups.

How does he sort the objects?

What might be Aiden's sorting rule?

Background Information for Teachers

Prior to having students solve this problem, give them the opportunity to explore 3-D objects. Allow time for students to manipulate, observe, and discuss the objects, as well as to identify characteristics.

Have students use the three-dimensional objects template (included in the Appendix on page 248) to sort objects and describe their rules.

Think

Talk

Solve
Students may use various sorting rules. For example:
- One set of objects can roll, one set of objects cannot roll.
- One set of objects has corners, one set of objects does not.
- Objects in one set are larger, objects in the other set are smaller.

Share

Extend
Challenge students to find and collect 3-D objects from home, and create a class display. Examples include soup tins, tissue or cracker boxes, and so on).

Routine Problems

Date: _____ Name: _____

Aiden Sorts Three-Dimensional Objects

Aiden is sorting three-dimensional objects:

He puts 10 objects into 2 groups.

How does he sort the objects?

What might be Aiden's sorting rule?

Think

Talk

Solve

Share

39A

40A | Earl Collects Tins of Soup

Math Topic

Geometry

Math Conocpt

Three-dimensional objects

Problem

Earl is collecting tins of soup for the food bank.

He has 6 tins of tomato soup and 3 tins of chicken-noodle soup.

How many circles are on all of Earl's tins?

Background Information for Teachers

In order to approach this problem with confidence, students will benefit from previous exploration of three-dimensional objects—in particular, cylinders. To scaffold this problem, challenge students to identify 3-D objects in the environment, as well as the 2-D shapes found within them.

Note: Having a class scavenger hunt is a fun and beneficial way to help familiarize students with 2-D shapes and 3-D objects.

Before they begin solving this problem, ensure that students know where to find all the circles on the illustration. They might not think to include the bottom of the tin (which they cannot see) or the lid.

Students may use a variety of strategies to solve this problem, such as the following:

- Use manipulatives: 3-D solids or actual soup tins.
- Draw pictures of the soup tins, and count the circular faces.
- Use background knowledge that there are 2 circular faces on each tin, and then skip count by 2s.

Think

Talk

Solve

There are 18 circle faces altogether.

Share

Extend

Provide students with this extension problem:

How many rectangle faces are there on 3 tissue boxes?

Routine Problems

Date: _____   Name: _____

Earl Collects Tins of Soup

Earl is collecting tins of soup for the food bank.

He has 6 tins of tomato soup and 3 tins of chicken-noodle soup.

How many circles are on all of Earl's tins?

Think

Talk

Solve

Share

40A

Non-Routine Problems

Implementation of Non-Routine Problems

Non-routine problems are more challenging than routine problems for students to solve. Upon first reading, the path to a solution is not immediately evident. Students draw on a bank of strategies (teacher-presented and student-developed) to solve the problem. Possible strategies include

Grade 1 Strategies
1. **Act it out/use materials**
2. **Draw a picture/diagram**
3. **Look for a pattern**
4. **Use logical reasoning**
5. Guess and check
6. Make an organized list
7. Make a table
8. Work backwards
9. Use an equation
10. Use simpler numbers

Some non-routine problem-solving strategies are more appropriate for use at specific grades than others. The first four strategies listed above are introduced, taught, and practised in the grade 1 *Hands-On Problem-Solving* program. However, both students and teachers may discover opportunities to use the other six strategies as well. For this reason, all 10 strategies are described below:

1. Act it out/use materials

This strategy has students acting out the problem either with other students in the class or with manipulative materials. Students need to be aware that when acting out a problem (or using materials to do so) alternate objects can be substituted in place of the real items. For example:

There are 6 children playing ice hockey at the rink.

How many skates are the children wearing altogether?

To act out this problem with manipulatives, students might use interlocking cubes linked in pairs to represent the pairs of skates. Alternatively, they could act out the problem by counting their shoes to represent the ice skates.

2. Draw a picture/diagram

Drawing a picture or a diagram helps students better understand the problem they are trying to solve. Once they have read the problem they must then decide how to represent the information in picture or diagram form so that they can work through to a solution. The drawing can help to clarify some of the details of the problem for students.

It is important for students to understand that pictures or diagrams that mathematicians make are not detailed. They should be simple sketches and should not take a long time to draw. For example:

Marc, Jenny, Mason, and Ian are lining up for recess.

How many different ways can they line up?

For this problem, students could draw four simple stick figures on paper squares and label them with the names of the four students, as in the figure below. They could then move around the squares to show the various lineups.

3. Look for a pattern

With this strategy students look for a pattern in the problem and then use it to predict what will come next. Students must analyze the information in the problem and then use it to make predictions or generalizations.

For example:

Susan is knitting a scarf for her sister, Heather.

Heather's favourite colours are blue, brown, and green.

Susan knits a pattern of stripes on the scarf.

The part of the pattern that repeats is *blue, brown, blue, green*.

If Susan repeats this pattern 4 times, how many stripes does she knit?

For this problem, students could use crayons to draw the pattern, or they could use coloured cubes to create it. By repeating the pattern 4 times, students can determine the number of stripes knitted.

4. Use logical reasoning

This strategy involves the use of deductive reasoning. The strategy can support students in problem situations where they are given information that they need to use in order to eliminate possible solutions. These problems have students using an "if–then" approach. It is important that students read the entire problem before attempting to use this strategy so that they can choose the best clue(s) to help them solve the problem and discount other clues that are not helpful. Using a chart or drawing a picture can help students organize the information in these problems. For example:

Jacob and his 2 cousins, Jenny and Joey, are going swimming with their families.

Children 6 years old and under swim for free at Duck Street pool.

Use the clues to figure out who will swim for free, and who has to pay to get in:

Jacob is 3 years older than his cousin, Jenny.

Jenny is 5 years old.

Joey is 2 years younger than Jacob.

Students can use logical reasoning to solve this problem by beginning with what they do know: that Jenny is 5 years old. Jenny does not have to pay. If Jacob is 3 years older than Jenny, students can add 5 + 3 to find out Jacob's age. They can use similar reasoning to find out Joey's age and determine if the other two children have to pay or not.

Note: Although the following strategies are focused on at higher grade levels of the *Hands-On Problem-Solving* program, there may be opportunities to explore these with grade 1 students.

5. Guess and check

With this strategy students are encouraged to make a reasonable guess and then check to see if the potential answer fits the problem. This strategy requires persistence, because it often does not lead to an immediate solution. Incorrect guesses can give clues to the solution however.

It is important that students record their guesses along with their results so that they can see the patterns in order to find the solution. For example:

Mrs. Stevenson is planting her flower garden.

She plants 12 flowers.

She plants the same number of yellow flowers as white flowers.

She plants twice as many orange flowers as yellow flowers.

How many of each colour of flower does she plant?

To use this strategy, students might record a guess-list like the following:

Guess: 5 yellow   5 white   10 orange   **Check**: No

Guess: 4 yellow   4 white   8 orange   **Check**: No

Guess: 2 yellow   2 white   4 orange   **Check**: No

Guess: 3 yellow   3 white   6 orange   **Check**: Yes!

▶

Non-Routine Problems

Note, however, that grade 1 students would not be expected to create guess-and-check lists such as this—this strategy targets students at higher grade levels.

6. Make an organized list

Students can use this strategy when a problem has a great deal of information. Making an organized list helps to organize the data in order to see the relationships and patterns within it. For example:

You have 95¢ in your pocket.

What coins might you have?

Give as many solutions as you can.

Because there are a number of possible solutions to this problem, an organized list can help students to keep their thinking methodical and under control. The beginnings of an organized list for this data might look something like this:

1. 25¢ + 25¢ + 25¢ + 10¢ + 10¢ = 95¢
2. 25¢ + 25¢ + 25¢ + 10¢ + 5¢ + 5¢ = 95¢
3. 25¢ + 25¢ + 25¢ + 5¢ + 5¢ + 5¢ + 5¢ = 95¢
4. 25¢ + 25¢ + 25¢ + 10¢ + 5¢ + 1 + 1 + 1 + 1 = 95¢
5. 25¢ + 25¢ + 25¢ + 10¢ + 1 + 1 + 1 + 1 + 1 + 1 + 1 + 1 + 1 + 1 = 95¢

and so on. Note, however, that grade 1 students would not be expected to create organized lists such as this—this strategy targets slightly older students.

7. Make a table

Students can use this strategy when a problem includes data with more than one characteristic. Organizing the information in a table can help students to identify patterns or to find missing data. This strategy is often used with problems that involve logical reasoning or probability.

For example:

At the corner grocery store popsicles cost 50¢, ice cream bars cost 60¢ and fudge bars cost 80¢.

If you spend $6.00 on these treats, what could you buy?

List all the possibilities.

Popsicles – 50¢	Ice Cream Bars – 60¢	Fudge Bars – 80¢	Total
4 ($2.00)	4 ($2.40)	2 ($1.60)	$6.00
2 ($1.00)	4 ($1.80)	4 ($3.20)	$6.00
	and so on		

8. Work backwards

Students can use this strategy when a problem gives the results of an action and asks about something that happened earlier (in the beginning). Students have to think about the actions in reverse order. For example:

Amy tells Joel to think of a number but not say it out loud.

Then she asks him to add 10 to the number, then double that sum, and finally to subtract 5.

Joel's final answer is 45.

What number did Joel start with?

9. Use an equation

To use this strategy students can record an equation or equations to model the situation(s) in the problem. For example:

Hans has $1.64.

He has an equal number of pennies, nickels, dimes and quarters.

How many coins does he have in all?

10. Use a simpler or similar problem

Students can use this strategy when a problem has large numbers, lots of information, or many conditions. Creating a simpler problem can help students discover the way to solve the more

▶

complex problem. Sometimes a problem can be divided into simpler problems that, when looked at together, will lead to the solution. For example:

- In a book with 568 pages, how many 6s would you use to number the pages?

- Two bakers can make two fancy cakes in two days.

    How many cakes can 8 bakers working at the same rate make in 20 days?

There is more than one way to solve a problem!

Some non-routine problems can have more than one solution. Others can be solved using a variety of strategies. For example:

- There are 5 flowers in the basket. If the flowers are pink, yellow, and lavender, how many of each colour of flower could there be? Find all the combinations. (draw a diagram, use materials, act it out)

- Farmer Green sees some cows and geese in his yard. Altogether he counts 8 heads and 28 legs. How many cows does he see? How many geese does he see? (guess and check, draw a picture, use materials)

- The hotel restaurant has 25 small tables to use for large groups.

    Each table can seat only one person on each side.

    If all the tables are pushed together, how many people can sit at the long table? (draw a diagram, make a table, look for a pattern, use simpler numbers)

Teaching Non-Routine Problems

The grade 1 *Hands-On Problem-Solving* program focuses on four strategies: Act it out/use materials; Draw a picture/diagram; Look for a pattern; and Use logical reasoning. To introduce each strategy and to provide students with practice using each one, the problems are organized in the following manner:

Problems 1B–5B: Act it out/use materials

Problems 6B–10B: Draw a picture/diagram

Problems 11B–15B: Look for a pattern

Problems 16B–20B: Use logical reasoning

Problems 21B–40B: These can be solved using a variety of strategies, but no one strategy is suggested. Having students solve these problems independently will allow them to evaluate, select, and use the various problem-solving strategies taught and focused on with preceding problems.

Each non-routine problem-solving task provides the following information for teachers:

Problem-Solving Strategy: This indicates the specific strategy focused on in the problem. The first 20 non-routine problems are intended for instruction and introducing students to the various problem-solving strategies. For problems 21B to 40B students may choose themselves, from amongst the different strategies already learned, which one will help them to solve the problem. The intent is also to show students that a variety of different strategies can be used to solve a given problem.

Problem: The problem is stated in grade appropriate language and reading level. In addition, to support beginning grade 1 students, many of whom will be emerging readers, activity sheets for the first 13 problems are presented in rebus format, meaning that some words are displayed with pictorial representations. These illustrations, however, are not displayed on the corresponding lesson plans for teachers.

Background Information for Teachers: In this section, teachers may be provided with guidance regarding basic mathematical knowledge, vocabulary, or skills students will

▶

need in order to solve the problem; tips or specific pointers for presenting the problem to students; and other fact of interest.

Suggestions for scaffolding and introducing related concepts may also be provided.

In order to promote differentiated instruction and meet the needs of various learners, it is important to provide the necessary supports that students might need to solve a problem. For example, some students may choose to use manipulatives, while others may draw pictures, use symbols, or use a calculator. Ensure that these materials are available to students as needed.

Think: Providing "think" time ensures that students have adequate opportunity to read the problem, identify important information, and consider possible strategies for solution. Once a problem has been presented to students, it is important to allow this think time before asking them to share their ideas. Both in teacher lesson plans and on student activity sheets throughout the non-routine problems, the "Think" step is identified with the icon shown above.

Talk: As noted earlier, the process of communication is an essential element of mathematics and is one of the Big Ideas in Mathematics presented in the *Hands-On Problem-Solving* program. Once students have been given a problem and provided with time to think about it, the next step is to have them share their ideas as teachers probe their thinking with critical questions. Both in teacher lesson plans and on student activity sheets throughout the first 20 non-routine problems, the "Talk" step is identified with the icon shown above.

Note: As with the routine problems, it is important to stress that the questions included in the Talk section are provided for guidance and scaffolding. With the first 20 non-routine problems specific strategies are introduced and "Talk" questions are provided in more detail. For problems 21 to 40, students are encouraged to approach the tasks with more independence, posing questions themselves and using background knowledge, skills, and strategies to solve the problems. As such, there is no "Talk" section provided with problems 21 to 40.

Solve: As with the routine problems, in this section of each teacher lesson plan (problem), the correct response to the problem is provided. Students are expected to record their answer to the problem in the "solve" section on the corresponding activity sheet. Have students also record their strategies with their solutions, being sure to name their answer as well. Both in teacher lesson plans and on student activity sheets throughout the non-routine problems, the "Solve" step is identified with the icon shown above.

Share: As with the routine problems, students should be given time to share their strategies and solutions. This is an integral part of learning problem-solving skills, as students learn new strategies from one another. Honouring students' responses, whether right or wrong, can lead to opportunities for healthy mathematical discussions that create a learning environment where all can feel they have a voice and can take risks as learners. The role of the teacher as faciltator is crucial during this sharing session to ensure that each student's mathematical understanding is progressing and that misconceptions are not perpetuated. Both in teacher lesson plans and on student activity sheets throughout the non-routine problems, the "Share" step is identified with the icon shown above.

Assessment for, as, and of Learning:
Suggestions for assessment are provided throughout the non-routine problems section. Assessment *for* learning suggestions are provided particularly in cases where students require background skills in order to succeed with a given problem. In most cases, assessment *of* learning suggestions are provided with the last problem that focuses on each strategy, in order to identify student progress on a given strategy. Assessment *as* learning suggestions are provided sporadically with problems 21 to 40, to offer students the opportunity to reflect on their learning and choice of strategies.

Assessment is focused on in more detail in the ***Hands-On Problem Solving*** Assessment Plan (see pages 13-24).

Non-Routine Problem-Solving Activity Sheet:
A corresponding student activity sheet correlates with each problem-solving task provided in the teacher lesson plan. Each activity sheet supports students in the problem-solving process by presenting the problem followed by the guiding cues ("Think", "Talk", "Solve", and "Share") and matching picture icons. There is also space for students to show their solving strategies.

Students may work independently on these activity sheets, with partners or in small groups, or teachers may choose to read through the problems together with students and to complete them in large group settings. Activity sheets can also be made into overheads, projected onto a screen using a document camera, or recreated on chart paper.

Student completion of the activity sheets fosters development of communication skills in mathematics and can also be used as evidence of essential learning related to the problem-solving process.

Non-routine problem-solving activity sheets for problems 1 to 20 use the same format as routine problems: Problem, Think, Talk, Solve, and Share. For problems 21 to 40, the "Talk" section is eliminated, as the intent is for students to complete these problems independently.

An Additional Resource for Solving Non-Routine Problems

As students and teachers explore non-routine problem-solving strategies, they may find it helpful to reflect upon the various strategies taught and learned. For this purpose, a blackline master has been included (please see next page) that presents the non-routine problem-solving strategies on which students focus in grade 1. The blackline master can be photocopied onto sturdy tag board and laminated for long-term use. Teachers may choose to use this resource during lessons, as they support students in their problem solving. Students can glue their cards into problem-solving file folders or notebooks, or they can place the cards on desks or tables for use during problem-solving activities.

Non-Routine Problems

Blackline Master to Guide and Support Learning – Non-Routine Problems

Problem-Solving Strategies

- Draw a picture or diagram.

- Look for a pattern.

- Act it out/use materials.

- Use logical reasoning.

1B | Saving Money for the Pet Shelter

Problem-Solving Strategy

Act it out/use materials.

Problem

Tim is saving money to give to the pet shelter.

He has 10 cents.

Which coins might Tim have?

Is there more than one answer?

Background Information for Teachers

The non-routine problem-solving strategy suggested with this problem has students acting out the problem either with other students or with manipulative materials. Students need to be aware that alternate objects can be substituted for the real objects when they are acting out the problem to help them solve it.

To approach this problem with confidence, students will benefit from previous exposure to the names and values of the penny, the nickel, and the dime. Students will also need experience using coins to count by 1s, by 5s, and by 10s. Have real or play coins available for students to use while solving the problem.

To support students' literacy skills, read the problem aloud as students read along.

Assessment for Learning

Provide students with coins. Have them identify each coin by name and value, and have them practise using the coins to count by 1s, 5s, and 10s. Observe their choice of coins (when asked to identify a given coin) and their ability to count using the manipulatives.

Think

Talk

Discuss the problem with students. Ask:

- What do we need to find out? (what coins Tim might have)
- What do we know? (Tim has 10 cents.)
- What strategy could you use to solve the problem? (Students may suggest drawing a picture, which is a valid strategy. It is important to stress that various strategies may be used to solve any given problem. In this case, however, it is still important to introduce students to the suggested strategy, so approach this specific task using materials.)
- What materials could we use to help us solve the problem?

Provide students with coins, and then ask:

- How many different ways can we use coins to make 10 cents?

As each coin combination is suggested and validated, record these solutions on chart paper. Guide students in confirming the various combinations.

Solve

There are 4 possible answers: Tim could have 1 dime, 2 nickels, 10 pennies, or 1 nickel and 5 pennies.

Share

Non-Routine Problems

Date: _____   Name: _____

Saving Money for the Pet Shelter

Tim is saving money to give to the pet shelter.

He has 10 cents.

Which coins might Tim have?

Is there more than one answer?

Think

Talk

Solve

Share

1B

2B | Comparing Sunny and Rainy Days

Problem-Solving Strategy

Act it out/use materials.

Problem

The grade one class wants to know how many more sunny school days than rainy school days there were in October.

They look at the classroom calendar.

There were 7 rainy days and 12 sunny days.

How many more sunny days were there?

Background Information for Teachers

Calendars are often used in classrooms for discussions and learning about weather, making this problem particularly relevant in this context, and providing students with an opportunity to compare sets.

To approach this problem with confidence and understanding, students will benefit from experience with the concept of comparing sets and the term *more than*. Have manipulatives, such as blocks, available for students to use to solve the problem. They may act out the problem by making one row of blocks for rainy days and lining up another row for sunny days underneath it. This will allow students to compare the number of days and determine how many more of them were sunny.

Think

Talk

Discuss the problem with students. Ask:

- What do we need to find out? (how many more sunny days than rainy days there were in October)
- What do we know? (There were 7 rainy days and 12 sunny days.)
- What strategy could you use?

Have students share their ideas. They may suggest drawing pictures or using calendar weather cards. Ask:

- What materials can we use to solve the problem?

Before explaining how to act out the problem by comparing sets of blocks (as described in the Background for Teachers section), encourage students to think about and discuss how they could use materials to act out the problem. Have them share their ideas, then, guide them through the set-comparison process described previously.

Solve

There were 5 more sunny days than rainy days during the month of October.

Share

Non-Routine Problems

Date: _____   Name: _____

Comparing Sunny and Rainy Days

The grade one class wants to know how many more sunny school days than rainy school days there were in October.

They look at the classroom calendar.

There were 7 rainy days and 12 sunny days.

How many more sunny days were there?

Think

Talk

Solve

Share

3B Trading Stickers

Problem-Solving Strategy

Act it out/use materials.

Problem

Jade and Tammy both have sticker collections.

They are trading stickers.

Jade has 9 puppy stickers, and Tammy has 5 puppy stickers.

How many stickers must Jade give Tammy for them to have an equal number of puppy stickers?

Background Information for Teachers

This problem provides an appropriate follow-up to the preceding calendar problem. Use of manipulatives with this problem makes the transfer of stickers visual for students, as in the example below. Students must compare the number of stickers each girl has and then move some of the manipulatives to make both rows equal.

Jade   ○○○○○○○○○
Tammy ○○○○○

Transfer
Jade   ○○○○○○○⚬⚬
                    ↙↙↙
Tammy ○○○○○⚬⚬

Think

Talk

Discuss the problem with students. Ask:

- What do we need to find out? (how many puppy stickers Jade must give Tammy so they have an equal number of puppy stickers.)
- Have we done a problem like this before where we compared sets? (yes, the rainy and sunny days)
- What information do we know for this problem? (Jade has 9 puppy stickers, and Tammy has 5.)
- What strategy could you use to solve the problem?
- How could we use materials to help us solve the problem?
- What kinds of materials might we use?

Before explaining how to act it out by comparing sets and then transferring some stickers, ask students how they think the problem could be acted out. Guide them in creating sets, comparing sets, transferring, and ensuring equivalent sets.

Solve

Jade must give Tammy 2 stickers for the girls to have the same number of puppy stickers (7).

Share

Non-Routine Problems

Date: _____   Name: _____

Trading Stickers

Jade and Tammy both have sticker collections.

They are trading stickers.

Jade has 9 puppy stickers, and Tammy has 5 puppy stickers.

How many stickers must Jade give Tammy for them to have an equal number of puppy stickers?

Think

Talk

Solve

Share

4B | Game Bags for Number Cubes

Problem-Solving Strategy

Act it out/use materials.

Problem

The grade one class uses number cubes to play math games.

Their teacher, Ms. Higgins, wants to make game bags with 3 cubes in each bag.

There are 18 cubes.

How many bags can she make?

Background Information for Teachers

This problem provides an opportunity for students to explore sharing to make equal sets. Students will need access to manipulatives to solve the problem. If available, use number cubes and clear bags so students can see the sets.

Think

Talk

Discuss the problem with students. Ask:

- What do we need to find out? (how many game bags can be made if 3 cubes go into each bag)
- What information do we know? (There are 18 cubes.)
- What strategy could you use to help you solve the problem?
- How could we use materials to help solve the problem?
- What materials might we use?

Using manipulatives, guide students in showing how the cubes can be grouped in sets of 3. First, have students count out 18 cubes. Then, take 3 cubes at a time, and put them into the bags until all the cubes have been used.

Solve

Ms. Higgins can make 6 game bags.

Share

Non-Routine Problems

Date: _____   Name: _____

Game Bags for Number Cubes

The grade one class uses number cubes to play math games.

Their teacher, Ms. Higgins, wants to make game bags with 3 cubes in each bag.

There are 18 cubes.

How many bags can she make?

Think

Talk

Solve

Share

5B Picking Apples for Pies

Problem-Solving Strategy

Act it out/use materials.

Problem

In autumn, Danny picks apples from his apple tree.

He wants to bake some apple pies.

Danny collects 20 apples.

He uses 5 apples in each pie.

How many apple pies can he make?

Background Information for Teachers

This is another problem that encourages students to create equal sets. Use of real apples and pie plates will engage students in the problem-solving process. As an alternative, counters and containers can be used.

Think

Talk

Discuss the problem with students. Ask:

- What do we need to find out?
- Does it remind you of another problem we have solved? (Yes, we must make equal groups like the number cubes/game-bag problem.)
- What information do we know?
- What strategy could you use to help you solve the problem?
- How could you use materials to help solve the problem?
- What materials might you use?

Guide students in using manipulatives to show how the apples can be arranged in groups. Have students count out 20 "apples," and then group them in sets of 5 on the "pie plates" until all the apples have been grouped.

Solve

Danny can make 4 pies with 20 apples.

Share

Assessment of Learning

Conference with students individually. Have them explain how they used the act it out/use materials strategy to solve this problem. Record observations on copies of the Individual Student Observations sheet, found on page 17.

Non-Routine Problems

Date: _____   Name: _____

Picking Apples for Pies

In autumn, Danny picks apples from his apple tree.

He wants to bake some apple pies.

Danny collects 20 apples.

He uses 5 apples in each pie.

How many apple pies can he make?

Think

Talk

Solve

Share

6B Hat and Mitten Combinations

Problem-Solving Strategy

Draw a picture/diagram.

Problem

One snowy winter day, Coral wants to go outside.

She needs to wear a hat and mittens.

Coral has a pair of black mittens and a pair of yellow mittens.

She has a purple hat and a blue hat.

What are the different hat-and-mitten combinations Coral can wear?

Background Information for Teachers

The non-routine problem-solving strategy suggested with this problem involves drawing a picture or diagram, which helps students better understand the problem. They must read the problem and then decide how to represent the information in picture or diagram form so they can work through to a solution. Help students understand that the pictures/diagrams that mathematicians make are not detailed. They should be simple and quick to draw.

To help support students' literacy skills, read the problem aloud, or read it together as a class. Use chart paper and coloured markers (black, yellow, purple, and blue) to model drawings. Also provide students with blank paper and black, yellow, purple and blue crayons. Guide students as they discuss and solve the problem.

Think

Talk

Discuss the problem with students. Ask:

- What do we know?
- What do we need to find out?
- Do we know what choices Coral has? (She has black and yellow mittens and purple and blue hats.)
- How can we find out the answer? (Draw a picture of each hat and each pair of mittens.)
- How can we show the choices? (Draw each combination, or draw a line between pictures to show combinations.)

When presenting a new strategy to students, such as the "Draw a picture/diagram" strategy suggested in this lesson, it is recommended that teachers model each solution for them. For example, draw the black mittens with a purple hat, and ask:

- Which other hat could Coral wear with the black mittens?

Draw the black mittens and a blue hat. Ask:

- Are there any other hats Coral could wear?
- Are there any other mittens Coral could wear?

Draw the yellow mittens. Ask:

- Which hat could Coral wear with the yellow mittens?

Draw the yellow mittens with each hat to show the solution.

Solve

Coral can wear 4 possible hat-and-mitten combinations:

- Purple hat and black mittens
- Purple hat and yellow mittens
- Blue hat and black mittens
- Blue hat and yellow mittens.

Share

Non-Routine Problems

Date: _____   Name: _____

Hat and Mitten Combinations

One snowy winter day, Coral wants to go outside.

She needs to wear a hat and mittens.

Coral has a pair of black mittens and a pair of yellow mittens.

She has a purple hat and a blue hat.

What are the different hat-and-mitten combinations Coral can wear?

Think

Talk

Solve

Share

7B Making Aliens

Problem-Solving Strategy

Draw a picture/diagram.

Problem

Darcy wants to make some aliens for his space picture.

He wants each alien to be different.

He has paper triangles and circles for the bodies and paper rectangles for the legs.

He wants some aliens to have 2 legs and some aliens to have 3 legs.

How many different aliens can Darcy make?

Background Information for Teachers

Using chart paper to model drawings will be beneficial for students, as they may retain and refer to the strategy later when they encounter a similar problem.

Provide students with paper and pencils or whiteboards, dry-erase markers, and erasers.

Read the problem aloud to students, and have them read along. Introduce and review vocabulary as necessary.

Some students might benefit from manipulating the shapes to make their own aliens. A shapes template is included at the end of the lesson (see page 145) for this purpose.

Think

Talk

Discuss the problem with students, and ask:

- What do we need to find out?
- Does this problem remind you of another problem we have solved?
- What strategy could we use to help solve the problem? (Some students will make the connection to the mitten and hat problem. If not, pose more questions to help students relate the two problems.)
- What information is important for solving the problem?
- Is this like the choices Coral had between mittens and hats? How?
- Could we use the same strategy to help solve the problem? What is the strategy?

Model students' ideas on chart paper as they work on whiteboards or paper.

Once you have made all the necessary drawings, ask students:

- Have we solved the problem?
- Have all the possible aliens been made?

Solve

Darcy can make 4 different aliens:

- Triangle body and 2 rectangle legs
- Triangle body and 3 rectangle legs
- Circle body and 2 rectangle legs
- Circle body and 3 rectangle legs

Share

Non-Routine Problems

Date: _____   Name: _____

Making Aliens

Darcy wants to make some aliens for his space picture.

He wants each alien to be different.

He has paper triangles and circles for the bodies and paper rectangles for the legs.

He wants some aliens to have 2 legs and some aliens to have 3 legs.

How many different aliens can Darcy make?

Think

Talk

Solve

Share

7B

Shapes Template (Alien Body Parts)

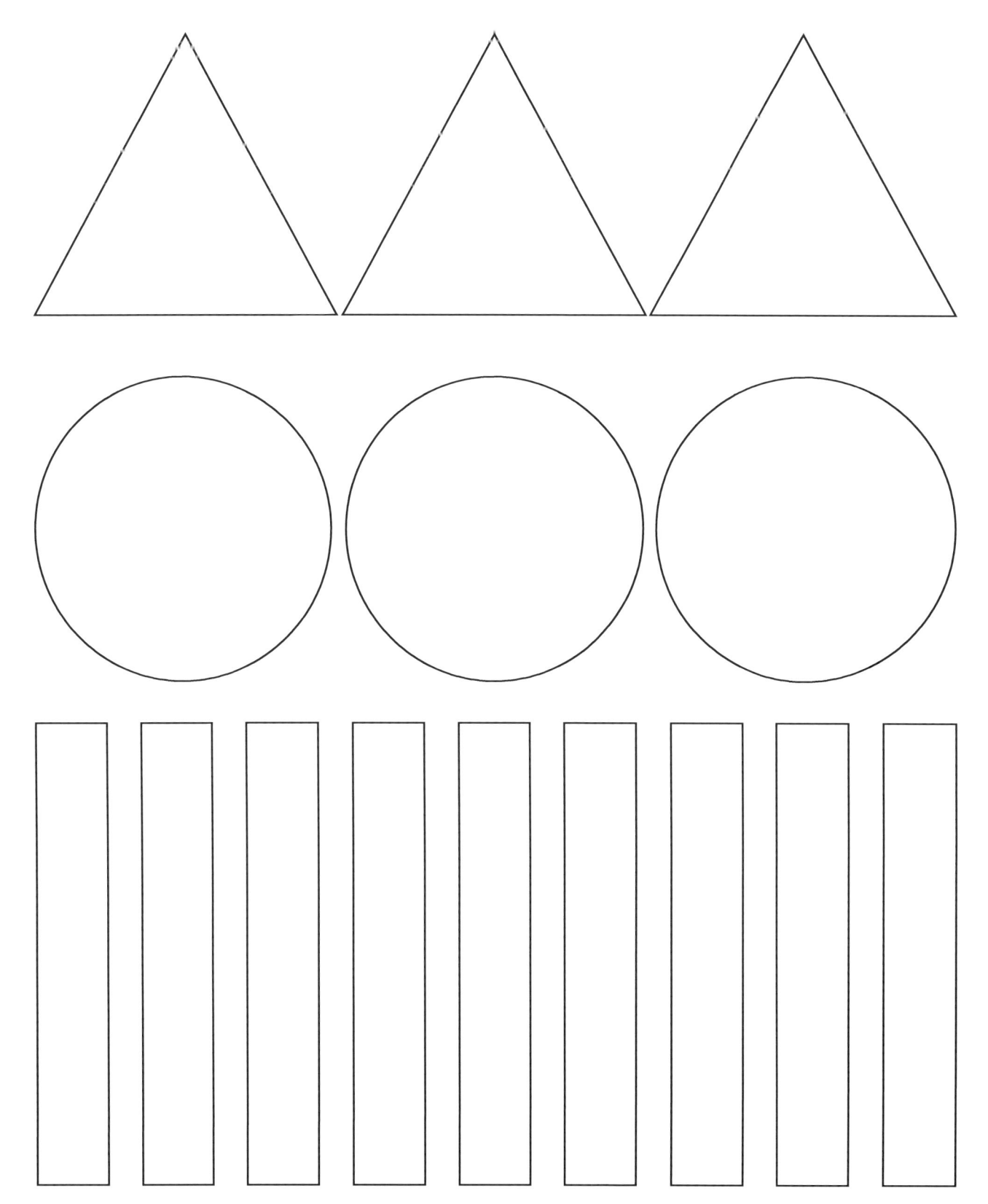

7B

8B Counting Robins and Spiders

Problem-Solving Strategy

Draw a picture/diagram.

Problem

One summer day José is watering his garden.

He sees spiders and robins in the garden.

He sees 4 heads and 20 legs.

How many spiders and robins does José see?

Background Information for Teachers

Use chart paper or a whiteboard to model the problem-solving process for students.

Provide students with paper and pencils or whiteboards, dry-erase markers, and erasers.

Note: This type of problem is also fun to do in the fall, substituting pigs and turkeys for the spiders and robins, or in the winter, substituting polar bears and snowy owls.

Think

Talk

Discuss the problem with students. Ask:

- What do we need to find out?
- What can we do to solve this problem?

Have students share their ideas for ways to solve the problem. If they do not mention drawing a picture, suggest that this is a possible strategy for solving this problem. Ask:

- How many animals are there altogether?
- How do you know?

Begin by drawing the four heads. Ask:

- How can we figure out how many of the heads are robin heads and how many are spider heads?
- How many legs are there on a robin?
- How many legs are there on a spider?
- Do both spiders and robins have at least 2 legs?
- Can we draw 2 legs on all the animals to start?

Some students may say "no," because a spider has 8 legs. It is important to explain that this is the beginning of the picture, and they will be adding more to it later. This represents the number of legs that the animals have in common.

Draw two legs on each of the four heads, and ask:

- How many legs have we drawn?
- What animals does our picture show?
- What other animals are in the problem?
- How many legs are in the problem?
- What can we do to include spiders in the picture?

Add six more legs to one of the heads. Continue adding legs to create spiders as students count on from 12 (2 + 2 = 4 for the two robins' legs, and then + 8 to add the first spider's legs), stopping as each spider is completed to remind students that the problem says that there are 20 legs altogether.

When you reach 20 legs, identify how many spiders and robins are in the picture (2 spiders and 2 robins).

Review the steps taken to solve the problem, and record these steps. Recording a phrase for each drawing as the problem is solved will allow for easier review. For example:

1. Draw a circle body for each animal.
2. Draw the legs that both animals have in common.
3. Add legs to make a third animal, counting until the total number of legs is reached.
4. Count the number of each animal.

Solve

José sees 2 spiders and 2 robins.

Share

Date: _____   Name: _____

Counting Robins and Spiders

One summer day José is watering his garden.

He sees spiders and robins in the garden.

He sees 4 heads and 20 legs.

How many spiders and robins does José see?

Think

Talk

Solve

Share

8B

9B | Playing on a Number Line

Problem-Solving Strategy

Draw a picture/diagram.

Problem

Dean is playing a game on a number line.

He places his counter at 0 on the number line.

He rolls a 3 on a number cube and jumps forward 3 times.

He rolls a 4, and then he rolls a 6.

Finally, he rolls a 5.

He jumps forward with very roll of the number cube.

On which number does Dean end up?

|+—+|
0 1 2 3 4 5 6 7 8 9 10 11 12 13 14 15 16 17 18 19 20

Background Information for Teachers

The number line is a valuable tool for solving problems. It allows students to visualize a process and solve a problem by counting forward and backward, or making jumps along the number line.

Think

Talk

Discuss the problem with students. Ask:

- What do we need to find out?
- What strategy could we use to help solve the problem?
- What information is important to solving the problem? (starts at 0; rolls a 3; jumps forward 3; rolls a 4, a 6, and a 5; always jumps forward)

On chart paper or a whiteboard, model the process of making jumps along the number line. Ask:

- What number does Dean roll first? (3)
- What does this 3 tell us to do? (Jump ahead 3.)
- What number does he roll next? (4)
- What does the 4 tell us to do? (Jump ahead 4.)

Have students continue on their own number lines to solve the problem.

Solve

Dean ends up on 18.

Share

Playing on a Number Line

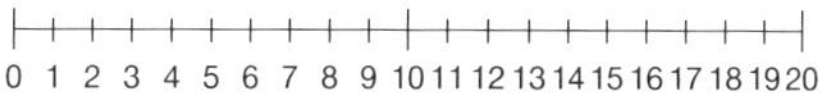

0 1 2 3 4 5 6 7 8 9 10 11 12 13 14 15 16 17 18 19 20

Dean is playing a game on a number line.

He places his counter at 0 on the number line.

He rolls a 3 on a number cube and jumps forward 3 times.

He rolls a 4, and then he rolls a 6.

Finally, he rolls a 5.

On which number does Dean end up?

Think

Talk

Solve

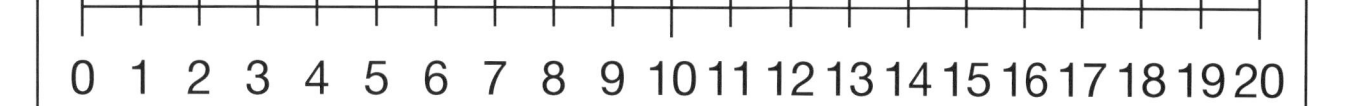

0 1 2 3 4 5 6 7 8 9 10 11 12 13 14 15 16 17 18 19 20

Share

9B

10B | Petals on Flowers

Problem-Solving Strategy

Draw a picture/diagram.

Problem

Sasha picks some flowers from his garden.

He picks 3 flowers.

Each flower has 6 petals.

Then Sasha picks off 1 petal from each flower.

How many petals are left on the flowers?

Background Information for Teachers

This problem is especially conducive to the draw a picture/diagram strategy, as it involves several steps and includes very visual concepts that are simple for most students to draw. Provide students with paper and pencils or whiteboards and markers to draw their pictures.

Think

Talk

Discuss the problem with students. Ask:

- What do we need to find out?
- What strategies could we use to help us solve the problem?

Have students share their ideas. Then, explain that drawing a picture can help you to solve the problem, because you can draw the flowers with the petals, count the flowers and petals, and remove (cross out) petals. Ask:

- How many flowers does Sasha pick? (Draw the 3 flower stems.)

Note: Some students might be disconcerted to see you draw just three stems, without flower head and petals. Ask them to be patient, and to use their imaginations and let the stems represent or stand for the whole flowers for just a few moments.

- How many petals are on each flower (Draw 6 petals on each flower.)
- How can we show that Sasha picks off some of the petals? (Cross them out.)

Now, have students draw their own flowers and petals, and complete the problem.

Solve

There are 15 petals left on the flowers.

Share

Assessment of Learning

Observe students as they use the draw a picture/diagram strategy to solve this problem. Also review students' activity sheets. Record your observations on copies of the Anecdotal Record sheet found on page 16.

Date: _____ Name: _____

Petals on Flowers

Sasha picks some flowers from his garden.

He picks 3 flowers.

Each flower has 6 petals.

Then Sasha picks off 1 petal from each flower.

How many petals are left on the flowers?

Think

Talk

Solve

Share

10B

151

11B | Painting the Fence

Problem-Solving Strategy

Look for a pattern.

Problem

Alexi's dad is painting the fence.

He paints the boards in an *AB* pattern.

He uses yellow and blue paint.

He has 8 boards to paint.

The first board is yellow.

How many of the 8 boards will be blue?

Background Information for Teachers

Looking for a pattern will help students to make sense of problem information. Practice extending patterns and identifying number of elements will help students to understand the problem. To support them as they solve the problem students may use blocks to represent the boards, or they may draw pictures.

Think

Talk

Discuss the problem with students. Ask:

- What do we need to find out?
- What information do we know?
- Does the pattern help us to solve the problem?

Have students use yellow and blue cubes to build the pattern. Then, guide them in using the pattern to determine how many of the boards will be blue.

Solve

There will be 4 blue boards.

Share

Painting the Fence

Alexi's dad is painting the fence.

He paints the boards in an *AB* pattern.

He uses yellow and blue paint.

He has 8 boards to paint.

The first board is yellow.

How many of the 8 boards will be blue?

Think

Talk

Solve

Share

12B A Pattern for Days of School

Problem-Solving Strategy

Look for a pattern.

Problem

The grade one class makes a pattern with shapes to show the number of days they have been in school.

The part of the pattern that repeats is *triangle, circle, square.*

The pattern begins on the first day of school.

What is the shape on the 10th day of school?

Background Information for Teachers

Reviewing pattern vocabulary with students and applying it to actual patterns will be important to their understanding of the problem. Review with students terms such as

- *Shape*
- *Triangle*
- *Circle*
- *Square*
- *Repeating pattern.*

Students may find it helpful to use a number line, included in the Appendix on page 244, while they are working at solving this problem.

Think

Talk

Discuss the problem with students. Ask:

- What do we need to find out?
- What information do we know?

Highlight the second line of the problem in some way, and ask students:

- What does the word *repeats* mean? (continues, goes on and on)
- What part of the pattern repeats? (triangle, circle, square)

Explain that the part of a pattern that repeats is called the *core.* Ask:

- Does the pattern help you to solve the problem?
- What strategy could you use?
- What materials might you use to help you solve the problem?

Students may recognize that a number line would be a helpful tool to use to solve the problem. Have them draw the shape pattern above the numbers on the number line until they reach 8. This will help to determine the solution.

Solve

The shape on the 10th day of school is a triangle.

Share

Assessment of Learning

Conference with students individually, and have each student explain how he or she used the look for a pattern strategy to solve this problem. Record your observations on copies of the Individual Student Observations sheet found on page 17.

A Pattern for Days of School

The grade one class makes a pattern with shapes to show the number of days they have been in school.

△ ○ □

The part of the pattern that repeats is *triangle, circle, square.*

The pattern begins on the first day of school.

What is the shape on the 10th day of school?

Think

Talk

Solve

Share

12B

13B Making a Keychain With Beads

Problem-Solving Strategy

Look for a pattern.

Problem

Monique is using beads to make a keychain.

She is using yellow, blue, and green beads.

This is how she puts them on the string:

yellow, blue, yellow, green, yellow, blue, yellow, green, yellow, blue, yellow, green, yellow, yellow, blue, green, yellow, blue, yellow green

Can you find Monique's mistake?

Background Information for Teachers

Experience creating and extending patterns as well as identifying the pattern core will be useful to students for solving this problem. Activities sorting correct and incorrect patterns can help students to identify pattern cores. To scaffold this, create several correct and incorrect pattern trains or bead chains. Have students examine them and sort them as correct or incorrect.

Students should have access to cubes or pattern blocks to model the problem. Recreating the pattern and lining up the core vertically will provide a visual to show the error.

Think

Talk

Discuss the problem with students. Ask:

- What do we need to find?
- What information do we know?
- What strategy could we use to solve this problem?
- Do you see a pattern?

Have students read the pattern aloud.

- What is the part of the pattern that repeats? (*yellow, blue, yellow, green*)

Explain to students that the part of a pattern that repeats is called the *core*. Have students use a crayon to highlight the core of the pattern on their activity sheets. Ask:

- Can we use the core to help us solve the problem?

Guide students in identifying the repeating core to find the mistake.

Solve

Monique's mistake is that "yellow, yellow, blue, green" (the fourth repetition of the pattern) should be "yellow, blue, yellow, green."

Share

Date: _____   Name: _____

Making a Keychain With Beads

Monique is using beads to make a keychain.

She is using yellow, blue, and green beads.

This is how she puts them on the string:

yellow, blue, yellow, green, yellow, blue, yellow, green, yellow, blue, yellow, green, yellow, yellow, blue, green, yellow, blue, yellow green

Can you find Monique's mistake?

Think

Talk

Solve

Share

13B

14B Toads Eating Flies

Problem-Solving Strategy

Look for a pattern.

Problem

Some toads are sitting in the grass.

A little toad eats 2 flies.

A second toad eats 4 flies.

A third toad eats 6 flies.

If this pattern continues, how many flies will the fifth toad eat?

Background Information for Teachers

The non-routine problem-solving strategy suggested for this problem involves looking for a pattern and then using it to predict what will come next. Students need to analyze the information in the problem and then make predictions or generalizations.

Students need to have experience with counting by 2s to solve this problem. Grade 1 students may not have had any formal experience with ordinal numbers. Use the following activities to review ordinal vocabulary (*first* through *fifth*):

- Have students work with different coloured interlocking cubes, placing them in sequence according to your instructions:
    - Put the red cube first, the yellow cube second, and the green cube third.
    - Choose another colour for fourth and fifth position.
    - Which cube is third? First? Fifth?
- Have students use manipulatives, such as cubes or counters, or draw pictures to create the pattern depicted in the story.

Read the problem aloud to students, and have them read along. Use chart paper to model solutions as needed.

Assessment for Learning

To assess students' abilities to count by 2s, have them work in groups to count feet, hands, eyes, and ears. To assess students individually, have them snap together several pairs of interlocking cubes and demonstrate counting by 2s.

Think

Talk

Discuss the problem with students. Ask:

- What do we need to find out?
- What do we know? (The first toad eats 2 flies, the second toad eats 4 flies, and the third toad eats 6 flies.)
- What strategy could we use to solve the problem? (Students may suggest drawing a picture, which may, in fact, help them to visualize and confirm the pattern.)
- Do you see a pattern? What is it?
- How can you use the pattern to solve the problem?

Have students either draw the pattern or use manipulatives to make it. Model this on chart paper as students make their own patterns. Ask:

- How many flies does the fourth toad eat?

It is important for students to note that the next number in the counting sequence (8) is not the answer, since this is only the fourth toad. Ask:

- How many flies does the fifth toad eat?

Solve

The pattern is 2, 4, 6, 8, 10.

The fifth toad eats 10 flies.

Share

Date: _____   Name: _____

Toads Eating Flies

Some toads are sitting in the grass.

A little toad eats 2 flies.

A second toad eats 4 flies.

A third toad eats 6 flies.

If this pattern continues, how many flies will the fifth toad eat?

Think

Talk

Solve

Share

14B

15B Clarence the Clown's Magic Bag

Problem-Solving Strategy

Look for a pattern.

Problem

Clarence the Clown has a magic bag.

He puts 2 candies into the bag and 4 candies come out.

He puts 3 balls into the bag and 6 balls come out.

He puts 4 cookies into the bag and takes 8 cookies out of the bag.

What will happen if Clarence puts 5 apples into the bag?

Background Information for Teachers

Experience with doubles to 10 will assist students in identifying the pattern. Some students may require cubes and a paper bag to model the problem.

Think

Talk

Discuss the problem with students. Ask:

- What do we need to find out?
- What information do we know?
- What is happening in the problem?
- Do you see a pattern?
- What is the pattern?
- Will the pattern help us to solve the problem?

Have students either use cubes to build the pattern or act out each step with a paper bag and cubes. For example

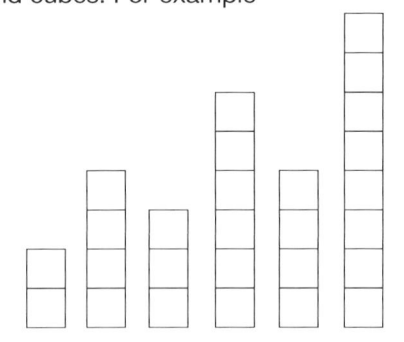

Guide students in using the pattern to determine the next number out of the bag.

Solve

If Clarence puts 5 apples into the bag 10 apples will come out.

Share

Date: _____   Name: _____

Clarence the Clown's Magic Bag

Clarence the Clown has a magic bag.

He puts 2 candies into the bag and 4 candies come out.

He puts 3 balls into the bag and 6 balls come out.

He puts 4 cookies into the bag and takes 8 cookies out of the bag.

What will happen if Clarence puts 5 apples into the bag?

Think

Talk

Solve

Share

15B

16B A Pattern With Blocks

Problem-Solving Strategy

Use logical reasoning.

Problem

There are 4 shapes of attribute blocks in a tub at the block centre.

Tanya wants to make a pattern using the same shape of block in different colours.

She chooses blocks that have:

- Corners
- Equal sides
- 4 sides.

Which blocks does Tanya choose for her pattern?

Background Information for Teachers

The non-routine problem-solving strategy suggested with this problem involves using logical and deductive reasoning. In this type of problem situation students are given information that they must use in order to eliminate possible solutions. These problems have students using an *if-then* approach.

It is important that students read the entire problem so they can decide what info is useful to them and what is not before beginning the problem.

Consider doing this problem as a class to model eliminating blocks that do not fit all of the attributes. Go through the list of attributes one at a time with students, and eliminate blocks that do not have that specific attribute. This is an effective introduction to logical reasoning using manipulatives and pictures.

In order for students to approach this problem with confidence and understanding, experience with attribute blocks through sorting activities and games will make visualization of the blocks easier. During such activities it is important to use, and encourage students to use, geometry vocabulary to describe the blocks, including terms such as *square, triangle, circle, round, corners, sides,* and *equal.*

Have attribute blocks available to students while they are working to solve this problem.

After solving the problem, play a related game with students. Have each student choose one attribute block. Orally present various block attributes, one at a time. Have students who have blocks that match that attribute hand in their shapes. This can be done as a process for lining up for recess, gym, and other out-of-class activities. As students hand in their shapes, they can join the line.

Think

Talk

Discuss the problem with students. Ask:

- What do we need to find out?
- What information do we know?
- How might we solve the problem?

Have students share their ideas. Explain that one strategy for solving the problem is to sort the blocks and remove those that don't fit with the clues given. Have students examine various attribute blocks (or the illustration on their activity sheet). Ask:

- Which blocks have corners?
- Which block can we remove?

16B

Have students cross out or remove the circle. Ask:

- Which blocks have 4 sides?
- Which block can we remove?

Have students cross out or remove the triangle. Ask:

- Which blocks have 4 equal sides?
- Which block can we remove?

Have students cross out or remove the rectangle. Ask:

- Which shape fits all of the attributes?

Solve

Tanya chooses to use square blocks for her pattern.

Share

Non-Routine Problems

Date: _____   Name: _____

A Pattern With Blocks

There are 4 shapes of attribute blocks in a tub at the block centre.

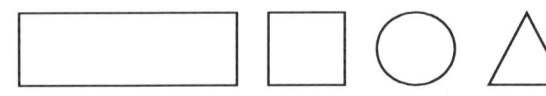

Tanya wants to make a pattern using the same shape of block in different colours.

She chooses blocks that have:

- Corners
- Equal sides
- 4 sides.

Which blocks does Tanya choose for her pattern?

Think

Talk

Solve

Share

164   16B

17B Cam Chooses a Pet

Problem-Solving Strategy

Use logical reasoning.

Problem

Cam wants to buy a pet.

He is choosing between a bird, a cat, a dog, and a rabbit.

He chooses a pet that

- Is furry
- Has 4 legs
- Does not hop
- Cannot climb trees.

Which pet does Cam choose?

Background Information for Teachers

For this problem, students need to carefully examine each animal picture and also use their knowledge of these animals to identify Cam's choice.

Think

Talk

Discuss the problem with students. Ask:

- What is the problem asking?
- What information do we know?
- What strategy can we use to solve the problem? (Use logical reasoning to sort attributes, eliminate animals, and identify Cam's choice.)

Guide students in matching attributes to pets. They may choose to place a checkmark above each animal that matches an attribute, and an *X* above animals that do not. Practising this organized process of elimination will enable students to approach other similar problems.

Solve

Cam chooses a dog.

Share

Non-Routine Problems

Cam Chooses a Pet

Cam wants to buy a pet.

He is choosing between a bird, a cat, a dog, and a rabbit.

He chooses a pet that
- Is furry
- Has 4 legs
- Does not hop
- Cannot climb trees.

Which pet does Cam choose?

Think

Talk

Solve

Share

18B Lining Up

Problem-Solving Strategy

Use logical reasoning.

Problem

Jack, Eric, Leo, and Pat are lining up for gym class.

Pat is first and Leo is last.

Jack is between Pat and Eric.

Who is third?

Background Information for Teachers

Students' familiarity with ordinal numbers will be important to their understanding of the problem. Although the terms *first, second, third,* and *fourth* are part of most grade 1 students' everyday language and activities, be sure to review this vocabulary with them so that they can succeed with the problem. For example:

- Have students line up in groups of four or five and identify, by name, who is first, second, third, fourth, and fifth.
- Have students sequence coloured counters according to ordinal directions (place the red counter first, the green counter second, the blue counter third, and so on).

After solving the problem, have students create similar problems using the names of students in the class. These problems can be presented orally or in writing, and solved using various strategies identified in the "Talk" section.

Think

Talk

Discuss the problem with students. Ask:

- What do we need to find out?

This question is particularly important, because simply figuring out the order of the students in line does not answer the question. Highlighting the question for students will be helpful. Ask:

- What information do we know?
- How might we solve this problem?

Some students may choose to use manipulatives, such as coloured blocks, and assign a colour to each student's name. Others may simply use the first letter of each name to record possible solutions. Another possibility is to have students wear nametags and act out the problem. This discussion is important to develop a plan for future problem solving involving logical reasoning.

Solve

The lineup is Pat, Jack, Eric, Leo.

Eric is the third person in the line.

Share

Date: _____   Name: _____

Lining Up

Jack, Eric, Leo, and Pat are lining up for gym class.

Pat is first and Leo is last.

Jack is between Pat and Eric.

Who is third?

Think

Talk

Solve

Share

19B | Carl's Coloured Cow Counters

Problem-Solving Strategy

Use logical reasoning.

Problem

Carl lines up 5 coloured cow counters on the table.

They are red, green, yellow, purple, and blue.

- The green cow is last.
- The yellow cow is second.
- The red cow is between the blue cow and the green cow.

Where is the purple cow?

Background Information for Teachers

Provide students with coloured counters or, if these are not available, use coloured cubes or crayons as a suitable substitute for students who require manipulatives to solve the problem.

This problem provides another opportunity to review ordinal vocabulary.

Think

Talk

Discuss the problem with students. Ask:

- What do we need to find out?
- What information do we know?
- What can we do to solve this problem?

Some students may choose to use manipulatives such a coloured counters or cubes. Others may use the first letter of each colour to record possible solutions.

Solve

The lineup is purple cow, yellow cow, blue cow, red cow, green cow.

The purple cow is first.

Share

Non-Routine Problems

Date: _____   Name: _____

Carl's Coloured Cow Counters

Carl lines up 5 coloured cow counters on the table.

They are red, green, yellow, purple, and blue.

- The green cow is last.

- The yellow cow is second.

- The red cow is between the blue cow and the green cow.

Where is the purple cow?

Think

Talk

Solve

Share

19B

20B | Spring Party Snacks

Problem-Solving Strategy
Use logical reasoning.

Problem
In March, Ms. Munroe's class is having a party to celebrate the first day of spring.

There are snacks at the class party.

The snacks are cookies, popcorn, gummy worms, and grapes.

Marc, Maggie, Kim, and Amir each have a different snack:

- Marc is eating a salty snack.
- Maggie is eating fruit.
- Kim is eating candy.
- What is Amir eating?

Background Information for Teachers
This logical reasoning problem requires matching of the attributes to the snacks.

To support students' literacy skills, read the problem aloud, having students read along. Also, identify, highlight, and discuss attribute terminology so that students understand all descriptors.

Think
Talk
Discuss the problem with students. Ask:

- What do we need to find out? (what snack Amir is eating)
- What information do we know? (there are cookies, popcorn, gummy worms, and grapes. Marc is eating a salty snack; Maggie is eating fruit; Kim is eating candy. They all have a different snack.)
- How might we solve this problem?
- Is this problem like any other problem we have solved? (the problem in which Cam chooses a pet)
- There is no information about what Amir is eating. How can we find this out?

Students may highlight names and the attributes of snacks, then match these to snack pictures or words. The snack left at the end is the one Amir eats.

Solve
Marc is eating popcorn, Maggie is eating grapes, and Kim is eating gummy worms. Amir must be eating cookies.

Share
Assessment of Learning
Observe students as they use the logical-reasoning strategy to solve this problem. Also review their activity sheets. Record your observations on copies of the Anecdotal Record sheet found on page 16.

Non-Routine Problems

Date: _____   Name: _____

Spring Party Snacks

In March, Ms. Munroe's class is having a party to celebrate the first day of spring.

There are snacks at the class party.

The snacks are cookies, popcorn, gummy worms, and grapes.

Marc, Maggie, Kim, and Amir each have a different snack:

- Marc is eating a salty snack.
- Maggie is eating fruit.
- Kim is eating candy.
- What is Amir eating?

Think

Talk

Solve

Share

20B

21B | Rows of Shape Cookies

Problem

Mary is baking cookies for a family barbeque.

She makes different shapes of cookies.

She lines them up on a cookie sheet.

In each row, Mary puts the cookies in this pattern: *star, moon, bell, star, moon, bell.*

If Mary makes 2 more rows of cookies, how many more of each shape does she need?

Background Information for Teachers

Students may use a variety of strategies to solve this problem, such as the following:

- Draw a picture.
- Use materials, such as geoshapes or stickers.
- Look for a pattern.

Think

Solve

Mary will need 4 more of each shape of cookie.

Share

Non-Routine Problems

Rows of Shape Cookies

Mary is baking cookies for a family barbeque.

She makes different shapes of cookies.

She lines them up on a cookie sheet.

In each row, Mary puts the cookies in this pattern: *star, moon, bell, star, moon, bell.*

If Mary makes 2 more rows of cookies, how many more of each shape does she need?

Think

Solve

Share

21B

22B Animals in the Barn

Problem

On a class fieldtrip to a farm Anna sees 8 animals in a barn.

She sees goats and chickens.

She counts 20 legs

How many of each animal does Anna see in the barn?

Background Information for Teachers

Students may use a variety of strategies to solve this problem, such as the following:

- Use materials, such as animal sorts.
- Draw pictures of the animals.

Think

Solve

Anna sees 2 goats and 6 chickens.

Share

Non-Routine Problems

Animals in the Barn

On a class fieldtrip to a farm Anna sees 8 animals in a barn.

She sees goats and chickens.

She counts 20 legs.

How many of each animal does Anna see in the barn?

Think

Solve

Share

23B | Making a Paper Chain

Problem

Jack, Mia, Michel, and Emily make a paper chain to hang up for a Chinese New Year party.

The chain has 20 links.

- Jack makes 4 chain links.
- Emily makes 2 less links than Jack.
- Mia makes 2 more links than Jack.
- Michel makes 2 more links than Mia.

How many links does each child make?

Background Information for Teachers

Students may use a variety of strategies to solve this problem, such as the following:

- Use materials, such as paper links.
- Draw a picture.
- Act it out.

Think

Solve

Jack makes 4 links.
Emily makes 2 links.
Mia makes 6 links.
Michel makes 8 links.

Share

Non-Routine Problems

Making a Paper Chain

Jack, Mia, Michel, and Emily make a paper chain to hang up for a Chinese New Year party.

The chain has 20 links.

- Jack makes 4 chain links.

- Emily makes 2 less links than Jack.

- Mia makes 2 more links than Jack.

- Michel makes 2 more links than Mia.

How many links does each child make?

Think

Solve

Share

24B | A Pattern With Shapes

Problem

Jacob uses a triangle, a square, a circle, and a hexagon to make a shape pattern.

- The shape with no corners is first.
- The shape with 3 sides is second.
- The shape with 6 sides is not last.

What is the order of shapes in Jacob's pattern?

Background Information for Teachers

Students may use a variety of strategies to solve this problem, such as the following:

- Use logical reasoning.
- Use materials, such as geoblocks or attribute blocks.
- Draw a picture.

Think

Solve

The order of shapes in the pattern that Jacob makes is circle, triangle, hexagon, square.

Share

Non-Routine Problems

Date: _____   Name: _____

A Pattern With Shapes

Jacob uses a triangle, a square, a circle, and a hexagon to make a shape pattern.

- The shape with no corners is first.

- The shape with 3 sides is second.

- The shape with 6 sides is not last.

What is the order of shapes in Jacob's pattern?

Think

Solve

Share

24B

25B Canada Day Cupcakes

Problem

Brett has cupcakes at his Canada Day party.

His mom makes 18 cupcakes and puts them onto 5 plates.

Some plates have 3 cupcakes and some plates have 4 cupcakes.

How many plates with 4 cupcakes does Brett's mom use?

Background Information for Teachers

Students may use a variety of strategies to solve this problem, such as the following:

- Draw a picture.
- Use materials, such as paper plates and counters.

Think

Solve

Brett's mom uses 3 plates with 4 cupcakes (and 2 plates with 3 cupcakes).

Share

Assessment as Learning

Have students reflect on their experience solving this problem by completing copies of the Student Self-Assessment sheet found on page 18.

Non-Routine Problems

Canada Day Cupcakes

Brett has cupcakes at his Canada Day party.

His mom makes 18 cupcakes and puts them onto 5 plates.

Some plates have 3 cupcakes and some plates have 4 cupcakes.

How many plates with 4 cupcakes does Brett's mom use?

Think

Solve

Share

26B | Decorating With Flags

Problem

The grade one class is decorating the gym for tonight's concert.

They put up a row of flags.

The flags are arranged in a pattern in the school colours: green, blue, and white.

The part of the pattern that repeats is *green, blue, blue, white*.

They use 20 flags in total.

How many flags of each colour do the students use?

Background Information for Teachers

Students may use a variety of strategies to solve this problem, such as the following:

- Look for a pattern.
- Draw a picture.
- Use materials, such as construction paper.

Think

Solve

The students use 5 green flags, 10 blue flags, and 5 white flags.

Share

Non-Routine Problems

Date: _____   Name: _____

Decorating With Flags

The grade one class is decorating the gym for tonight's concert.

They put up a row of flags.

The flags are arranged in a pattern in the school colours: green, blue, and white.

The part of the pattern that repeats is *green, blue, blue, white*.

They use 20 flags in total.

How many flags of each colour do the students use?

Think

Solve

Share

27B Pizza Day Snacks

Problem

It is pizza day at school today!

Henrique, Theo, Matt, and Ian each have a different snack along with their pizza.

The snacks are potato chips, oatmeal-raisin cookies, pudding, and apples.

Use the clues below to find out what each boy has for a snack:

- Theo eats a salty snack.
- Henrique doesn't like raisins.
- Matt chooses fruit.

Background Information for Teachers

Students may use a variety of strategies to solve this problem, such as the following:

- Draw a picture.
- Use logical reasoning.

Think

Solve

Theo eats potato chips, Henrique eats pudding, Matt eats an apple, and Ian eats oatmeal-raisin cookies.

Share

Non-Routine Problems

Date: _____   Name: _____

Pizza Day Snacks

It is pizza day at school today!

Henrique, Theo, Matt, and Ian each have a different snack along with their pizza.

The snacks are potato chips, oatmeal-raisin cookies, pudding, and apples.

Use the clues below to find out what each boy has for a snack:

- Theo eats a salty snack.
- Henrique doesn't like raisins.
- Matt chooses fruit.

Think

Solve

Share

28B Making Repeating Patterns

Problem

The grade one class is using pattern blocks to make repeating patterns.

The part of Jonah's pattern that repeats is *red, blue, blue, orange*.

The part of Zoe's pattern that repeats is *yellow, green, blue*.

They both repeat their patterns 3 times.

How many of each colour block do Jonah and Zoe use altogether?

Background Information for Teachers

Students may use a variety of strategies to solve this problem, such as the folowing:

- Act it out.
- Draw a picture.
- Use materials, such as pattern blocks.

Think

Solve

Altogether Jonah and Zoe use 3 red blocks, 9 blue blocks, 3 orange blocks, 3 yellow blocks, and 3 green blocks.

Share

Non-Routine Problems

Date: _____   Name: _____

Making Repeating Patterns

The grade one class is using pattern blocks to make repeating patterns.

The part of Jonah's pattern that repeats is *red, blue, blue, orange.*

The part of Zoe's pattern that repeats is *yellow, green, blue.*

They both repeat their patterns 3 times.

How many of each colour block do Jonah and Zoe use altogether?

Think

Solve

Share

28B

29B Wrapping Presents

Problem

Jewel is wrapping presents for her grandmother's birthday.

She has red wrapping paper, blue wrapping paper, and pink wrapping paper.

She has white ribbon and silver ribbon.

How many different combinations of wrapping paper and ribbon can Jewel use to wrap the presents?

Background Information for Teachers

Students may use a variety of strategies to solve this problem, such as the following:

- Draw a picture.
- Use materials, such as coloured construction paper and wool.

Think

Solve

Jewel can use 6 different wrapping-paper and ribbon combinations:

Red wrapping paper with white ribbon
Red wrapping paper with silver ribbon
Blue wrapping paper with white ribbon
Blue wrapping paper with silver ribbon
Pink wrapping paper with white ribbon
Pink wrapping paper with silver ribbon.

Share

Non-Routine Problems

Wrapping Presents

Jewel is wrapping presents for her grandmother's birthday.

She has red wrapping paper, blue wrapping paper, and pink wrapping paper.

She has white ribbon and silver ribbon.

How many different combinations of wrapping paper and ribbon can Jewel use to wrap the presents?

Think

Solve

Share

30B Going for a Bike Ride

Problem

5 friends are going for a bike ride in the park.

Some are on bicycles, and some are on tricycles.

There are 13 wheels altogether.

How many friends are on bicycles and how many are on tricycles?

Background Information for Teachers

Students may use a variety of strategies to solve this problem, such as the following:

- Draw a picture.
- Use materials, such as counters, to represent the wheels.

Think

Solve

There are 2 friends on bicycles and 3 friends on tricycles.

Share

Assessment as Learning

Have students reflect on their thinking and strategies for solving this problem by completing copies of the Problem-Solving Journal sheet found on page 19.

Non-Routine Problems

Date: _____   Name: _____

Going for a Bike Ride

5 friends are going for a bike ride in the park.

Some are on bicycles, and some are on tricycles.

There are 13 wheels altogether.

How many friends are on bicycles and how many are on tricycles?

Think

Solve

Share

31B | Lindsey Plays a Board Game

Problem

Lindsey is playing a board game.

She is trying to get from "Start" to "Finish" in 5 moves.

First, she rolls a 6 on the number cube and moves ahead 6 spaces.

Then she rolls a 4, then a 1, then a 3, and then another 3.

Does Lindsey reach the finish line?

Background Information for Teachers

Students may use a variety of strategies to solve this problem, such as they following:

- Draw a picture or diagram (using the game board).
- Use a number line.
- Use materials (for example, counters).
- Act it out (with a number cube).

Think

Solve

No, Lindsey does not reach "Finish" in 5 moves.

She only gets to 17.

Share

Non-Routine Problems

Date: _____   Name: _____

Lindsey Plays a Board Game

Lindsey is playing a board game.

She is trying to get from "Start" to "Finish" in 5 moves.

First, she rolls a 6 on the number cube and moves ahead 6 spaces.

Then she rolls a 4, then a 1, then a 3, and then another 3.

Does Lindsey reach the finish line?

Think

Solve

Share

194   **31B**

32B Building Model Homes

Problem

The grade one class at Jackson School is building model homes in social studies.

They make the homes out of Plasticine.

1 bag of Plasticine makes 2 homes.

The students want to make 13 homes.

How many bags of Plasticine does the class need?

Will there be any clay left over when they are done?

Background Information for Teachers

Students may use a variety of strategies to solve this problem, such as the following:

- Draw a picture.
- Use materials, such as play dough, clay, or Plasticine.
- Act it out (have students put Plasticine, or a substitute, into bags, divide the contents of each bag into 2, and then count lumps of Plasticine to 13).

Think

Solve

The grade one class needs 7 bags of Plasticine.

There will be half a bag of clay left over.

Share

Non-Routine Problems

Date: _____   Name: _____

Building Model Homes

The grade one class at Jackson School is building model homes in social studies.

They make the homes out of Plasticine.

1 bag of Plasticine makes 2 homes.

The students want to make 13 homes.

How many bags of Plasticine does the class need?

Will there be any clay left over when they are done?

Think

Solve

Share

196   32B

33B | Juan Makes New Friends

Problem

Juan moves to Canada from Mexico.

He goes to a new school in Calgary.

He makes 17 new friends on Monday, 18 new friends on Tuesday and 19 new friends on Wednesday.

If this pattern continues, how many friends does Juan make on Friday?

Background Information for Teachers

Students may use a variety of strategies to solve this problem, such as the following:

- Draw a picture.
- Use materials, such as people sorts on a calendar.
- Look for a pattern.

Think

Solve

On Friday Juan makes 21 new friends.

Share

Non-Routine Problems

Date: _____   Name: _____

Juan Makes New Friends

Juan moves to Canada from Mexico.

He goes to a new school in Calgary.

He makes 17 new friends on Monday, 18 new friends on Tuesday and 19 new friends on Wednesday.

If this pattern continues, how many friends does Juan make on Friday?

Think

Solve

Share

34B | Tables for Students

Problem

The grade one class has 17 students.

The students sit at 5 tables for math centres.

Some tables have room for 4 students and some tables have room for 3 students.

How many tables have room for 3 students?

How many tables have room for 4 students?

Background Information for Teachers

Students may use a variety of strategies to solve this problem, such as the following:

- Use materials, such as plastic containers or sheets of construction paper (to represent tables) and counters or people sorts (to represent students).
- Draw a picture using white boards and dry-erase markers.

Think

Solve

There are 3 tables with 3 students and 2 tables with 4 students.

Share

Tables for Students

The grade one class has 17 students.

The students sit at 5 tables for math centres.

Some tables have room for 4 students and some tables have room for 3 students.

How many tables have room for 3 students?

How many tables have room for 4 students?

Think

Solve

Share

35B | Phillip's Toy Cars

Problem

Phillip is parking his toy cars in the car garage.

The cars are purple, red, yellow, green, and blue.

- The yellow car is in the middle.
- The blue car is behind the yellow car.
- The red car is second.
- The green car is not last.

What order are the cars parked in the garage?

Background Information for Teachers

Students may use a variety of strategies to solve this problem, such as the following:

- Use logical reasoning.
- Draw a picture.
- Use materials, such as coloured toy cars.
- Act it out (have students pretend to be the cars, holding coloured construction paper to represent colour).

Think

Solve

The green car is first.

The red car is second.

The yellow car is third.

The blue car is fourth.

The purple car is fifth (last).

Share

Assessment as Learning

Have students reflect on their experiences solving this problem by sharing thoughts and ideas with a classmate in an interview process.

Non-Routine Problems

Phillip's Toy Cars

Phillip is parking his toy cars in the car garage.

The cars are purple, red, yellow, green, and blue.

- The yellow car is in the middle.
- The blue car is behind the yellow car.
- The red car is second.
- The green car is not last.

What order are the cars parked in the garage?

Think

Solve

Share

36B | Monkeys on the Jungle Bus

Problem

The jungle bus picks up the monkeys for school.

It picks up 1 monkey at the first tree, 2 monkeys at the second tree, and 3 monkeys at the third tree.

The pattern continues.

After the fifth tree, how many monkey passengers are on the bus?

Background Information for Teachers

Students may use a variety of strategies to solve this problem, such as the following:

- Look for a pattern.
- Draw a picture.
- Use materials, such as animal sorts.
- Act it out (have students pretend to be monkeys getting on the bus).

Think

Solve

After the fifth tree there are 15 monkeys on the bus.

Share

Non-Routine Problems

Date: _____   Name: _____

Monkeys on the Jungle Bus

The jungle bus picks up the monkeys for school.

It picks up 1 monkey at the first tree, 2 monkeys at the second tree, and 3 monkeys at the third tree.

The pattern continues.

After the fifth tree, how many monkey passengers are on the bus?

Think

Solve

Share

37B | Coloured Bears on Numerals

Problem

Chloe is playing a game on the number line, using a red bear as the marker.

There are already other coloured bears on some numbers of the number line.

Chloe picks a number 5 card and puts the red bear on number 5 of the number line along with the orange bear.

Then she picks another card and has to go back 2 jumps to the blue bear.

The next card says to go ahead 4 jumps.

Now she moves the red bear to where the green bear is.

The next card says jump back 1.

There is no other bear on this number.

On which number is each bear?

Background Information for Teachers

Students may use a variety of strategies to solve this problem, such as the following:

- Act it out.
- Use materials, such as gummy bears and a number line.
- Draw a picture.
- Draw a number line.

Think

Solve

The orange bear is on 5.

The blue bear is on 3.

The green bear is on 7.

The red bear is on 6.

Share

Non-Routine Problems

Coloured Bears on Numerals

Chloe is playing a game on the number line, using a red bear as the marker.

There are already other coloured bears on some numbers of the number line.

Chloe picks a number 5 card and puts the red bear on number 5 of the number line along with the orange bear.

Then she picks another card and has to go back 2 jumps to the blue bear.

The next card says to go ahead 4 jumps.

Now she moves the red bear to where the green bear is.

The next card says jump back 1.

There is no other bear on this number.

On which number is each bear?

Think

Solve

Share

38B | Four Rabbits Race to a Carrot

Problem

Four rabbits are having a race to the big, orange carrot.

The rabbits are white, brown, black, and grey.

- The brown rabbit is second to the finish line, where the carrot is waiting.
- The white rabbit is right behind the brown rabbit.
- The grey rabbit is not last.

Which rabbit gets the carrot?

Background Information for Teachers

Students may use a variety of strategies to solve this problem, such as the following:

- Use logical reasoning.
- Draw a picture.
- Use materials, such as crayons to represent each rabbit.
- Act it out (have students pretend to be the rabbits, holding coloured construction paper to correspond with the colour of the rabbits).

Think

Solve

The grey rabbit gets the carrot.

(The brown rabbit is second.

The white rabbit is third.

The black rabbit is last.)

Share

Non-Routine Problems

Date: _____   Name: _____

Four Rabbits Race to a Carrot

Four rabbits are having a race to the big, orange carrot.

The rabbits are white, brown, black, and grey.

The brown rabbit is second to the finish line, where the carrot is waiting.

The white rabbit is right behind the brown rabbit.

The grey rabbit is not last.

Which rabbit gets the carrot?

Think

Solve

Share

39B | Shannon Builds a Clay-Cube Corral

Problem

Shannon is making a corral for her toy horses.

She makes cubes out of clay to build the fence.

She makes 15 cubes on Monday, 14 cubes on Tuesday, and on Wednesday she makes 13 cubes.

If this pattern continues, how many cubes does Shannon make on Thursday?

Background Information for Teachers

Students may use a variety of strategies to solve this problem, such as the following:

- Look for a pattern.
- Use materials to represent the clay cubes and fence (corral).
- Draw pictures of the clay cubes and fence (corral) each day.

Think

Solve

Shannon makes 12 cubes on Thursday.

Share

Non-Routine Problems

Shannon Builds a Clay-Cube Corral

Shannon is making a corral for her toy horses.

She makes cubes out of clay to build the fence.

She makes 15 cubes on Monday, 14 cubes on Tuesday, and on Wednesday she makes 13 cubes.

If this pattern continues, how many cubes does Shannon make on Thursday?

Think

Solve

Share

40B | How Many Children Are on the Play Structure?

Problem

The grade one class goes outside for recess.

15 children climb onto the play structure.

3 children leave the play structure to play on the swings, and 5 more climb onto the play structure.

Then, 4 children leave the play structure to go play soccer, and 1 more climbs back onto the structure.

How many children are on the play structure now?

Background Information for Teachers

Students may use a variety of strategies to solve this problem, such as the following:

- Act it out.
- Draw a picture.
- Use materials, such as people sorts and paper plates.

Think

Solve

There are 14 children on the play structure now.

Share

Assessment as Learning

Have students reflect on their experience solving this problem by completing copies of the Problem-Solving Journal sheet found on page 19.

Non-Routine Problems

Date: _____   Name: _____

How Many Children Are on the Play Structure?

The grade one class goes outside for recess.

15 children climb onto the play structure.

3 children leave the play structure to play on the swings, and 5 more climb onto the play structure.

Then, 4 children leave the play structure to go play soccer, and 1 more climbs back onto the structure.

How many children are on the play structure now?

Think

Solve

Share

Extended Exploration Problems

Implementation of Extended Exploration Problems

Extended exploration problems are meant to provide a thought-provoking challenge for students. These problems may present mathematical situations that are slightly beyond the grade-level curricular outcomes/expectations, may take the form of an investigation, or may require an extended period of time to solve. In all cases, students are encouraged to use their own strategies to arrive at a solution(s).

Extended problems are open-ended, can be investigative in nature, and have multiple entry points to allow for differentiation. They often

- Have more than one solution/answer
- Can be solved using a variety of strategies
- Require students to gather their own data
- Require creative and critical thinking
- Require more/extended time to solve
- Make connections to the real world.

Extended problems support the other six "big idea" mathematical processes: communication, connections, mental math, estimation, reasoning, technology, and visualization. The engaging nature of these problems helps students develop perseverance and critical thinking.

Examples of Extended Exploration Problems

- Bashira puts 12 red interlocking cubes onto one pan of the balance scale.
  Takami puts some blue and yellow interlocking cubes onto the other pan to balance the scale.
  List all the possible combinations of blue and yellow interlocking cubes that Takami could use to balance the scale.

- Maya is making hamburger patties for a family barbeque.
  She puts 24 patties onto a baking sheet. Show the different ways she could arrange the patties into equal groups.
  Which way is easiest to count?

- Use 20 pattern blocks to create a pattern.
  Trace your pattern onto paper.
  Give each pattern block a coin value (1¢, 5¢, 10¢, 25¢, $1.00 or $2.00).
  What is the value of your pattern?
  Can you make a pattern of lesser value? Greater value?

Teaching Extended Exploration Problems

Each extended exploration in the *Hands-On Problem-Solving* program provides the following information for teachers:

Problem: The problem is stated in grade-appropriate language and at a grade-appropriate reading level.

Math Topic: This indicates the connection to curricular strands, including number, patterns, geometry, measurement, data, probability, and variables and equations.

Math Concepts: This identifies mathematics skills and concepts focused on in the problem, based on the curricular outcomes/expectations.

Facilitating the Process: This section provides a description of the ways teachers can guide the problem-solving process, the kinds of activities students might be involved in, the materials they might choose to use, the strategies they might select, and how teachers can help those students who are struggling with the task.

Teachers can use the following procedures to guide students through the process of solving extended exploration problems:

1. Present the problem to students. Read the problem aloud to the class, or read it together as a class.

▶

2. Have students identify what the problem is asking. Make sure they understand what they are trying to find out, but do not discuss strategies. The goal is, rather, to encourage them to expose the mathematics so that strategies for solving the problem emerge naturally and logically. Instead of *telling* students the math, have them *construct* their learning under your guidance as their teacher.

3. Group students in pairs of similar ability as much as possible. This enables them to work at parallel levels of understanding and to approach the problem with comparable skills, concepts, and strategies.

4. Have manipulatives visible and accessible to students as needed. Do not, however, suggest which materials to use. Instead, encourage students to discuss the problem with their partners and identify, together, potential strategies and materials that could assist them in solving it.

5. Provide each pair with a large sheet of paper (chart or ledger) and two different colours of markers for recording their work and stages of thinking. Having students use markers rather than pencils ensures that all of their work is visible when they report back to the class. Having each student in the pair use a different colour of marker helps students identify their own work and contributions, and allows teachers to observe student engagement and contributions to the problem-solving process.

6. Have students find a workspace in the classroom and then discuss and select a strategy to solve the problem.

7. Circulate to observe what strategies and materials each group chooses and also to identify levels of thinking.

8. Scaffold only if a pair of students is struggling or unable to get started. It is seldom necessary to scaffold the problem for the whole class. Instead, work with pairs, asking focused questions to spark their thinking. Sometimes simply rereading the problem and identifying the question is enough to redirect. Teachers may also ask guided questions to assist struggling students with their choice of strategy.

9. Based on their needs and performance in problem solving, teachers may choose to differentiate problems for specific pairs of students, which may involve changing the level of difficulty of a problem to foster success while maintaining challenge. Suggestions for differentiating extended exploration problems are included throughout the **Hands-On Problem-Solving** program.

To support teachers as they facilitate the process just described, a template has been included on page 218, offering an abbreviated version of the steps listed above. This may serve as a useful resource for teachers when students are solving extended exploration problems. This template can be photocopied onto sturdy tag board and laminated for long-term use.

Note: After the first teacher lesson plan, details of this process that would repeat from problem to problem have not been included. For subsequent problems teachers are encouraged to follow the guidelines described with the first problem or to refer to the Facilitating the Process template. Lesson plans also include *new* details within this section, however, so it is important for teachers to review the section for every problem.

Extended Exploration Problems

Report, Debrief, and Consolidate Learning:
When all students have solved the extended exploration problem, collect student work. Sort the work samples based on the strategies students used.

Note: If time does not permit all pairs to share their work during the reporting and debriefing session, select samples that show a range of strategies for the class meeting described below.

Gather students together for a class meeting. As much as possible, encourage students to lead the discussion, by offering ideas, asking questions, and seeking clarification. This meeting should include the following steps:

1. Have students share solutions with the class by presenting and discussing their recorded work.

2. Encourage students to ask each other questions during presentations. To encourage higher-level thinking and questioning, prior to reporting and debriefing have the class brainstorm possible questions to ask each other. For example:

   - Why did you choose that strategy?
   - Why did you choose to use these materials?
   - Did you try any other strategies that didn't work?
   - Can you explain that again?

   Teacher modelling is important. If possible, model the questioning with another adult to present both questions and responses.

3. After groups have shared, help students identify and label strategies used, and make connections between strategies. Record this process on chart paper to refer to during future problem-solving activities.

To support teachers as the class reports and debriefs, a template has been included on page 218, offering an abbreviated version of the steps listed above. Once again, this may serve as a useful resource for teachers when students are solving extended explorations. This template can be photocopied onto sturdy tag board and laminated for long-term use. Teachers may also wish to photocopy this template back-to-back with the Facilitating the Process template, in order to have both resources together.

Note: Again, after the first teacher lesson plan, details of this process that would repeat from problem to problem have not been included. For subsequent problems teachers are encouraged to follow the guidelines described with the first problem or to refer to the Report, Debrief, and Consolidate Learning template. Lesson plans also include *new* details within this section, however, so it is important for teachers to review the section for every problem.

Solve: As with the routine and non-routine problems, in this section of each teacher lesson plan, the correct response to the problem is provided, when applicable.

Next Steps: This section offers suggestions for extensions to the original problem.

Extended Exploration Activity Sheet: The activity sheet includes the problem to be solved and, in some cases, illustrations or graphic organizers. Students should complete all their work on large sheets of paper, which can then be easily displayed later during the "Report, Debrief, and Consolidate Learning" process. Students will not show their solutions on the actual activity sheet.

During the process of solving an extended exploration problem, students are still encouraged to Think, Talk (with their partners), Solve (together, with their partners), and Share

▶

(Report, Debrief, and Consolidate Learning), so these icons are included on the student activity sheets:

- **Think**
- **Talk Together**
- **Solve Together**
- **Share**

Extended Exploration Problems

Blackline Masters to Guide and Support Learning – Extended Explorations

Extended Explorations – Facilitating the Process

1. Read the problem aloud or together.
2. Discuss what students need to find out, but do not discuss strategies.
3. Group students in pairs of similar ability.
4. Have manipulatives accessible to students as needed.
5. Provide each pair with a large sheet of paper and markers.
6. Have the pairs of students work independently to solve the problem and record their solutions.
7. Circulate to observe strategies and materials being used, and to identify levels of thinking.
8. Provide scaffolding only when a pair of students is struggling or is unable to get started.
9. Differentiate by revising problems or providing additional supports or challenges.

Encourage communication through the use of rich, probing questions and meaningful conversations with and among students.

Extended Explorations – Report, Debrief, and Consolidate Learning

1. Have students share their solutions and recorded work.
2. Encourage students to ask each other questions, seek clarification, and share ideas.
3. After all groups have shared, work together to identify and label strategies used, and make connections between strategies.

Encourage students to lead the discussion as they report, debrief, and consolidate their learning.

1C Sorting Bingo Chips

Math Topic

Number

Math Concepts

- Addition
- Making sets

Problem

The grade one class is sorting bingo chips into bags.

They have red, green, blue, and yellow bingo chips.

They want to put 1 chip of each colour into every bag.

There are 7 red chips, 6 green chips, 8 blue chips, and 7 yellow chips.

How many bags can they fill?

Facilitating the Process

For the extended exploration problems, it is important to keep in mind the following procedures:

1. Present the problem to students. Read the problem aloud to the class, or read it together as a class.

   Note: Many students in the earlier months of grade 1 will be emergent readers and will require support and guidance in reading and interpreting problems. Please refer to the section called Supporting Literacy During Problem Solving on page 8 of the Program Introduction.

2. Have students identify what the problem is asking. Make sure students understand what they are trying to find out, but do not discuss strategies. The goal is, rather, to encourage them to discover the mathematics so that strategies for solving the problem emerge. Instead of *telling* students the math, have them *construct* their learning under your guidance as their teacher.

3. Group students in pairs of similar ability whenever possible. This enables them to work at parallel levels of understanding and to approach the problem with comparable skills, concepts, and strategies.

4. Have manipulatives visible and accessible to students as needed. Do not, however, suggest which materials to use. Instead, encourage students to discuss the problem with their partners and identify, together, potential strategies and materials that could assist them in solving it.

5. Provide each pair with a large sheet of paper (chart or ledger) and markers, for recording their work and stages of thinking. (Have students use markers rather than pencils so that all of their work is visible when they report back to the class). Provide each student in the pair with a different colour of marker. This helps students identify their own work and contributions, and allows teachers to observe student engagement and contributions to the problem-solving process.

6. Have students find a workspace in the classroom and proceed in discussing and selecting a strategy to solve the problem.

7. Circulate to observe what strategies and materials each pair chooses and also to identify levels of thinking.

8. Scaffold only if a pair of students is struggling or unable to get started. It is seldom necessary to scaffold the problem for the whole class. Instead, work with groups, asking focused questions to spark their thinking. Sometimes simply rereading the problem and identifying the question is enough to redirect. Teachers may also ask guided questions to assist struggling students with their strategy choice.

9. Based on their needs and performance in problem solving, teachers may choose to differentiate problems for individual students, which may involve changing the level of difficulty of a problem to foster success while maintaining challenge.

Materials: Students may choose to use bags or containers, bingo chips or other coloured counters, paper, and crayons or markers to support them as they solve the problem.

Scaffolding: For students who require scaffolding, review the problem to ensure that they understand the task. Teachers can also guide students in making one bag of bingo chips in order to visualize the set.

To Differentiate: For students who require differentiation, teachers can use fewer (or more) colours of bingo chips to decrease (or increase) the level of difficulty (for example, use only two or three *colours* of chips rather than the four colours). As another option, teachers can use fewer (or more) total bingo chips to decrease (or increase) the level of difficulty (for example, use only 4 red chips, 3 green chips, 5 blue chips, and 4 yellow chips).

Report, Debrief, and Consolidate Learning

When all students have solved the extended exploration, collect student work. Sort the work samples based on the strategies students used.

Note: If time does not permit all groups to share their work during the reporting and debriefing session, select samples that show a range of strategies for the class meeting described below.

Gather students together for a class meeting. As much as possible, encourage students to lead the discussion by offering ideas, asking questions, and seeking clarification. This meeting should include the following steps:

1. Have students share solutions with the class by presenting and discussing their recorded work.

2. Encourage students to ask each other questions during presentations. To encourage higher-level thinking and questioning, prior to reporting and debriefing have the class brainstorm possible questions to ask each other. For example:

   - Why did you choose that strategy?
   - Why did you choose to use these materials?
   - Did you try any other strategies that didn't work?
   - Can you explain that again?

   Teacher modelling is important. If possible, model the questioning with another adult to present both questions and responses.

3. After groups have shared, help students identify and label strategies used, and make connections between strategies. Record this process on chart paper to refer to during future problem-solving activities.

Solve

The grade one students can fill 6 bags with 1 of each colour of bingo chip.

Next Steps

Have students solve the following problem:

How many more of each colour of bingo chip do the students need if they want to fill 4 *more* bags with 1 chip of each colour in every bag?

Note: Encourage all pairs to try this task. Observe which students use the data from their solution to the main problem or whether they begin again.

Sorting Bingo Chips

The grade one class is sorting bingo chips into bags.

They have red, green, blue, and yellow bingo chips.

They want to put 1 chip of each colour into every bag.

There are 7 red chips, 6 green chips, 8 blue chips, and 7 yellow chips.

How many bags can they fill?

- Think
- Talk Together 
- Solve Together 
- Share

2C Heads or Tails?

Math Topic
Number

Math Concepts
- Addition
- Mental math strategies

Problem
Miss Benhar gives Masani and Najja 12 nickels.

They place the nickels in a cup, shake the cup, and spill out the coins.

How many heads and how many tails might they see on the coins?

What are all the different number sentences they could make to fill the frame below?

_____ + _____ = 12

Facilitating the Process
Follow the guidelines described with the preceding problem on page 219–220 or refer to the Facilitating the Process template included on page 218.

Introduce students to the concepts of *heads* and *tails* by examining different coins, tossing them, and identifying how they land on heads or tails.

Materials: Students will need nickels to properly explore this problem. They may also choose to use a string of 12 beads or two-sided counters (to determine number sentences for 12) or a number line (included in the Appendix on page 244) to support them as they solve the problem.

Scaffolding: For students who require scaffolding, review the problem, ensuring they understand the task. Teachers can also guide students in determining one number sentence for 12, and then encourage them to find others.

To Differentiate: For students who require differentiation, use fewer (or more) nickels to decrease (or increase) the level of difficulty.

Some students will make a list of possible equations as they recognize the pattern: as the first digit increases by 1 the second digit decreases by 1 (for example, 1 + 11; 2 + 10).

Report, Debrief, and Consolidate Learning
Refer to the template on page 218 to guide the Report, Debrief, and Consolidate learning section. Have students share their strategies, written work, and solutions with you and their classmates.

Solve
Masani and Najja might see any of the following combinations of heads and tails on the coins:

0 (heads) + 12 (tails) = 12 (coins);
1 (heads) + 11 (tails) = 12 (coins);
2 (heads) + 10 (tails) = 12 (coins);
3 + 9 = 12;
4 + 8 = 12;
5 + 7 = 12;
6 + 6 = 12;
7 + 5 = 12;
8 + 4 = 12;
9 + 3 = 12;
10 + 2 = 12;
11 + 1 = 12;
12 + 0 = 12.

Next Steps
Have students record all the number sentences that fill this frame: 12 − _____ = _____.

2C

Note: To complete this task students can draw on their understanding of the part-part-whole concept. To solve the problem students can use addition equations to create the subtraction equations.

Heads or Tails?

Miss Benhar gives Masani and Najja 12 nickels.

They place the nickels in a cup, shake the cup, and spill out the coins.

How many heads and how many tails might they see on the coins?

What are all the different number sentences they could make to fill the frame below?

_____ + _____ = 12

Think

Talk Together

Solve Together

Share

3C | Making Mother's Day Bracelets

Math Topic

Patterns

Math Concepts

- Creating a pattern
- Making sets

Problem

The grade one students are making bracelets for Mother's Day.

Each bracelet has 3 different colours of beads.

The students use the same number of each colour of bead to make an *ABC* pattern.

Each bracelet has 24 beads.

Draw one of the bracelets to show the pattern.

How many of each colour is used on 1 bracelet?

Facilitating the Process

Follow the guidelines described with problem 1C on page 219–220 or refer to the Facilitating the Process template included on page 218.

Materials: Students may choose to use materials such as bingo chips, cubes, coloured markers, or actual beads to support them as they solve the problem.

Scaffolding: For students who require scaffolding, have them build the *ABC* core to visualize the pattern, then have them repeat the pattern, counting the beads until they reach 24.

To Differentiate: For students who require differentiation, use fewer beads or decrease the size of the pattern core to decrease the level of difficulty; or, use more beads or increase the size of the pattern core to increase the level of difficulty.

Report, Debrief, and Consolidate Learning

Follow the guidelines described with problem 1C or refer to the Report, Debrief, and Consolidate Learning template included on page 218.

Solve

There are many possible colour patterns students could create. Two examples are:

blue, yellow, white, blue, yellow, white...
(to 8 repetitions)

green, red, pink, green, red, pink...
(to 8 repetitions)

Next Steps

Have students show all the ways they could make an *ABBC* pattern using 24 beads in the same 3 colours as in the main problem.

Extended Exploration Problems

Date: _____   Name: _____

Making Mother's Day Bracelets

The grade one students are making bracelets for Mother's Day.

Each bracelet has 3 different colours of beads.

The students use the same number of each colour of bead to make an *ABC* pattern.

Each bracelet has 24 beads.

Draw one of the bracelets to show the pattern.

How many of each colour of bead is on the bracelet?

Think

Talk Together

Solve Together

Share

4C | Combinations of Blue and Yellow Cubes

Math Topic

Equality

Math Concepts

- Equality
- Addition

Problem

Jacques puts 15 red cubes into one bucket of the balance scale.

Max puts blue and yellow cubes into the other bucket to balance the scale.

How many cubes does Max use to balance the scale?

List all the possible combinations of blue and yellow cubes that Max could use to balance the scale.

Facilitating the Process

Materials: Students may choose to use materials such as bingo chips, cubes, or blocks and bucket-type balance scales to support them as they solve the problem.

Scaffolding: For students who require scaffolding, have them use the balance scale and cubes to explore equality. Ask students to place 10 cubes on one side of the scale and add 1 cube at a time to the other side of the scale until it balances. As another scaffolding option, have students place 12 cubes on one side of the scale and gradually add 2 colours of cubes to the other side until it balances. Then, ask students to count how many of each colour of cube there are.

To Differentiate: For students who require differentiation, decrease or increase the number of cubes on the scale.

Report, Debrief, and Consolidate Learning

When students share their solutions, watch for those who make the connection, without use of materials, to record reversed equations, such as 6 + 9 / 9 + 6.

Solve

Max uses 15 cubes on the other side of the scale to balance it.

Possible combinations of blue and yellow cubes that Max could use to balance the scale include

1 blue, 14 yellow

2 blue, 13 yellow

3 blue, 12 yellow

…

13 blue, 2 yellow

14 blue, 1 yellow.

Next Step

Have students place 15 cubes into one bucket of the scale, and use 3 different colours of cubes in the other bucket to balance the scale. Then, have students then create number sentences for the following frame:

____ + ____ + ____ = 15

Extended Exploration Problems

Date: _____   Name: _____

Combinations of Blue and Yellow Cubes

Jacques puts 15 red cubes into one bucket of the balance scale.

Max puts blue and yellow cubes into the other bucket to balance the scale.

How many cubes does Max use to balance the scale?

List all the possible combinations of blue and yellow cubes that Max could use to balance the scale.

- Think
- Talk Together 
- Solve Together 
- Share

5C | Grouping Cookies in Equal Sets

Math Topic
Number

Math Concept
Representing a number with equal groups

Problem
Mateo is baking cookies for a bake sale.

He puts 24 cookies onto a cookie sheet.

Show the different ways he could group the cookies in equal sets.

Which groups are the easiest to count?

Facilitating the Process
This problem connects well to the children's book, *The Doorbell Rang*, by Pat Hutchins, in which Ma makes a dozen cookies for her 2 children, but when the doorbell rings, more children arrive to share the cookies. Consider using this book as a springboard or follow-up to the problem solving experience.

Before students begin to solve this extended exploration problem, discuss the criteria for success, and have them share their ideas.

For example:

- Count total of 24 correctly
- Make equal groups
- Show more than one way to group the cookies
- Explain which groups are easiest to count, and why.

Have students refer to these criteria throughout the problem-solving process.

As students work in pairs to solve the problem, circulate to observe their strategies and thinking processes. Focus specifically on whether or not the pairs have a plan in place. If they are trying random strategies, ask them questions to help them generate a plan.

Materials: Students may choose to use materials such as construction paper or styrofoam trays (to represent the cookie sheets) and counters (to represent the cookies) to support them as they solve the problem.

Scaffolding: Have students who require scaffolding use counters and containers to divide the "cookies" into equal groups. This may help them to visualize the equal sets. They can then arrange the counters on the "cookie sheet" in the same manner. For example:

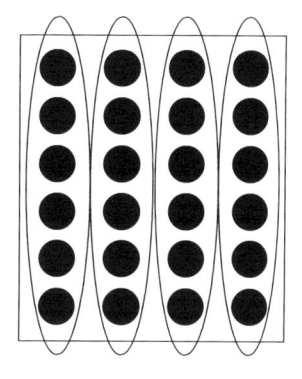

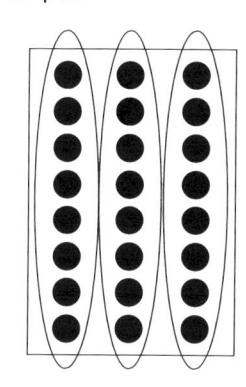

To Differentiate: For students who require differentiation, increase or decrease the number of cookies in the problem. Another option is to provide students with a frame for arranging the cookies, as in the following example:

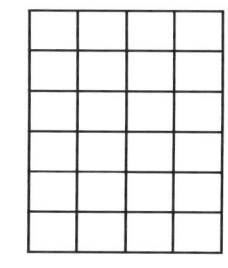

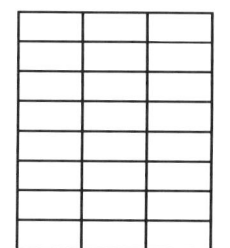

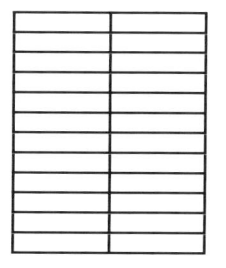

Extended Exploration Problems

5C

Report, Debrief, and Consolidate Learning

Solve

Mateo could arrange the cookies into 2 sets of 12 cookies, 12 sets of 2 cookies, 3 sets of 8, 8 sets of 3, 4 sets 6, or 6 sets of 4.

Groups of 2 are easiest to count.

Assessment of Learning

Record the criteria discussed above on copies of the Rubric sheet, found on page 21. Then, use the criteria to assess students' work.

Assessment as Learning

Students can use the same criteria described above to self-assess as well. Have them discuss the task with their partners and assess their own success according to the rubric criteria.

Next Steps

Have students solve the following problem:

If Mateo has 23 cookies, how can he arrange the cookies into equal groups?

How many cookies will be left over?

Date: _____   Name: _____

Grouping Cookies in Equal Sets

Mateo is baking cookies for a bake sale.

He puts 24 cookies onto a cookie sheet.

Show the different ways he could group the cookies in equal sets.

Which groups are the easiest to count?

- Think
- Talk Together
- Solve Together
- Share

6C | Plants for Mr. Green's Flower Pots

Math Topic
Number

Math Concepts
- Represent numbers
- Addition

Problem
Mr. Green wants to buy some plants for his flowerpots.

He decides to put 2 vines, 3 daisies, and 2 lilies into each pot.

Mr. Green has 4 flowerpots.

How many of each plant does he buy altogether?

Facilitating the Process

Materials: Students may choose to use materials such as links, bingo chips, and cubes (to represent the vines, daisies, and lilies, respectively), and tubs to represent the pots, in order to support them as they solve the problem.

Scaffolding: For students who require scaffolding, guide them in visualizing the problem, breaking it down into parts. Ask:

- How many vines are in each pot?
- How many vines are in 2 pots? 3 pots? 4 pots?

To Differentiate: For students who require differentiation, decrease (or increase) how many kinds of plants Mr. Green plants, or decrease (or increase) the number of flower pots.

Report, Debrief, and Consolidate Learning

Solve
Mr. Green buys 8 vines, 12 daisies, and 8 lilies altogether.

Next steps
Present the following problem to students:

Mr. Green decides to fill each of 4 more pots with 2 vines, 3 daisies, and 2 lilies. How many plants does he need to buy for all 8 pots?

Note: Having students complete this task provides information about whether they can simply double the numbers from their solution to the main problem or if they will recalculate again.

Date: _____   Name: _____

Plants for Mr. Green's Flower Pots

Mr. Green wants to buy some plants for his flowerpots.

He decides to put 2 vines, 3 daisies, and 2 lilies into each pot.

Mr. Green has 4 flowerpots.

How many of each plant does he buy altogether?

Think

Talk Together

Solve Together

Share

7C Rolling Number Cubes

Math Topic
Number

Math Concept
Addition

Problem
Use two number cubes that are numbered 1 to 6.

Roll both number cubes together 10 times.

Record the number sentence for each roll:

_____ + _____ = _____

What is the number sentence with the greatest sum?

What is the number sentence with the lowest sum?

Did you roll any doubles?

Facilitating the Process

Materials: Students will need 2 six-sided number cubes in order to explore this problem. Some students may also choose to use calculators, number lines, or counters in order to support them as they solve the problem (see the note about differentiating, below).

Scaffolding: For students who require scaffolding, first model several rolls of one number cube to demonstrate that there are different numbers on each side. Next, model one roll of the two number cubes, and have students record the numbers displayed as an equation. This will provide an example to help them complete the task.

To Differentiate: For students who require differentiation, have them use supports to calculate and/or check their number sentences. For example, they may choose to use calculators, number lines, counters, and so on.

Report, Debrief, and Consolidate Learning

Solve
Students' answers will vary for this problem.

Next Steps
- Have students repeat the problem using two number cubes that are numbered 1 to 9.
- Have students repeat the problem using three number cubes that are numbered 1 to 6.

Date: _____   Name: _____

Rolling Number Cubes

Use two number cubes that are numbered 1 to 6.

Roll both number cubes together 10 times.

Record the number sentence for each roll.

____ + ____ = ____

What is the number sentence with the greatest sum?

What is the number sentence with the lowest sum?

Did you roll any doubles?

Think

Talk Together

Solve Together

Share

8C Using A Non-Standard Measurement

Math Topic
Measurement

Math Concept
Non-standard measurement

Problem
Use a non-standard measurement such as a paperclip, toothpick, or interlocking cube.

Find 6 objects that are:

Less than 10 units long	Equal to 10 units long	Greater than 10 units long

Record your answers under the correct heading in the measurement chart provided.

Facilitating the Process
Students may choose to use any non-standard measurement available in the classroom. The variety of non-standard measurements selected will enhance the class discussion during the Report, Debrief, and Consolidate Learning session.

Be sure to model the process of using non-standard measurements for measuring. It is important to remember that the edge of the first unit must be placed exactly at the edge of the item that is being measured, and that units must be placed adjacent to one another, with no space between.

Another strategy is to use interlocking cubes or links to measure length. Since these are connected, they may be easier for some students to use for this task.

Materials: Provide students with copies of the activity sheet, which includes a measurement chart for them to record the objects that they find. Students will also need options for choosing their non-standard measurement in order to complete the problem.

Scaffolding: For students who require scaffolding, provide them with opportunities to explore linear measurement. For example, have them order items by length from shortest to longest. Or, provide students with a piece of string of a given length, and have them identify items shorter than, the same length as, and longer than the string.

To Differentiate: For students who require differentiation, change the numbers on the chart so that students are looking for, and measuring, objects with fewer (or more) units. For example, find 6 objects that are less than 1 unit in length, or 5 units, or 20 units.

Report, Debrief, and Consolidate Learning
As students share the data gathered on their charts, they will have an opportunity for comparison of the non-standard measurements used.

Solve
Students' answers will vary for this problem.

Next Steps
Have students exchange non-standard measurements and then measure the same objects as they did previously to observe the differences. For example, if a student used a paper clip as the non-standard measurement for the main problem, have him or her use a cube or a link.

Date: _____   Name: _____

Using Non-Standard Units of Measure

Use a non-standard measurement such as a paperclip, toothpick, or interlocking cube.

Find 6 objects that are:

Less than 10 units long	Equal to 10 units long	Greater than 10 units long

Record your answers under the correct heading in the chart provided.

Think

Talk Together

Solve Together

Less than 10 units long	Equal to 10 units long	Greater than 10 units long

Share

8C

9C Be a Shapes Detective!

Math Topic
Geometry

Math Concept
Identifying 2-D shapes and 3-D objects

Problem
Be a shapes detective!

Look for 2-D shapes and 3-D objects in magazines, newspapers, flyers, and anywhere else you can find them.

Find examples of six different 2-D shapes and six different 3-D objects.

Decide on a way to sort your pictures.

Glue the pictures onto a large sheet of paper, and label each group.

Facilitating the Process
Before students begin to solve this extended exploration problem, discuss the criteria for success, and have students share their ideas. For example:

- Find six 2-D shapes.
- Find six 3-D objects.
- Sort the pictures.
- Record sorting rules.

Have students refer to these criteria throughout the problem-solving process.

Materials: Provide students with poster paper (or chart paper, other large sheets of paper), scissors, glue, and markers. Gather together a collection of magazines, flyers, newspapers, wallpaper samples, and wrapping paper in (or on) which students can look for their 2-D shapes and 3-D objects. Also provide access to the Internet so that students can look for images online and print them out. As well, if digital cameras or iPads are available, students can look for 2-D shapes and 3-D objects in the school, on clothing, and so on and take photos of what they find.

Scaffolding: For students who require scaffolding, have them find 2-D shapes and 3-D objects on one wall of the classroom. Ask them to identify the shapes and objects by name.

To Differentiate: For students requiring differentiation, decrease or increase the number of shapes and objects students need to find. As another option, challenge students to find 2-D shapes and 3-D objects with which they are unfamiliar by name, and have them use research to determine their identity (for example, a parallelogram or a prism).

Solve
Students' answers will vary for this problem, depending on the 2-D shapes and 3-D objects they find and how they choose to organize (sort) them on their posters.

Report, Debrief, and Consolidate Learning
Give students time to share their discoveries with the rest of the class and to explain their groupings.

Assessment of Learning
Use copies of the Rubric sheet included on page 21 to record the criteria discussed above. Use these criteria to assess students' work.

Assessment as Learning
Students can use the criteria described above to self-assess as well. Have students discuss the task with their partners and assess their success according to the rubric criteria.

9C

Next Steps

Laminate students' completed posters, and cut apart the various examples of 2-D shapes and 3-D objects. Challenge students to sort the examples and explain their sorting rules.

Extended Exploration Problems

Date: _____ Name: _____

Be a Shapes Detective!

Be a shapes detective!

Look for 2-D shapes and 3-D objects in magazines, newspapers, flyers, and anywhere else you can find them.

Find examples of six different 2-D shapes and six different 3-D objects.

Decide on a way to sort your pictures.

Glue the pictures onto a large sheet of paper, and label each group.

Think

Talk Together

Solve Together

Share

10C Making Numbers

Math Topic

Number

Math Concept

Representing numbers

Problem

Sol says he can make all of the numbers from 1 to 20 using only the digits 1, 2 and 5 to make number sentences.

Is he right?

Facilitating the Process

Materials: Students may choose to use materials such as interlocking cubes to support them as they solve this problem. For example, they may construct interlocking-cube trains of 1, 2, and 5 in different colours for each number (for example, 1 = blue, 2 = yellow, 5 = green) as support.

Scaffolding: For students requiring scaffolding, use interlocking-cube trains to model the process.

To Differentiate: For students who require differentiation, decrease the range to 10 in order to decrease the level of difficulty, or increase the range to 30, in order to increase the level of difficulty.

Report, Debrief, and Consolidate Learning

Solve

Sol is right.

To make the numbers 1 through 20 Sol could make the following equations:

To make the number 1: $2 - 1 = 1$;

To make the number 2: $1 + 1 = 2$;

To make the number 3: $2 + 1 = 3$;

To make the number 4: $2 + 2 = 4$;

To make the number 5: $2 + 2 + 1 = 5$;

To make the number 6: $2 + 2 + 2 = 6$;

To make the number 7: $5 + 2 = 7$;

To make the number 8: $5 + 2 + 1 = 8$;

To make the number 9: $5 + 2 + 2 = 9$;

To make the number 10: $5 + 5 = 10$;

To make the number 11: $5 + 5 + 1 = 11$;

To make the number 12: $5 + 5 + 2 = 12$;

To make the number 13: $5 + 5 + 2 + 1 = 13$;

To make the number 14: $5 + 5 + 2 + 2 = 14$;

To make the number 15: $5 + 5 + 5 = 15$;

To make the number 16: $5 + 5 + 5 + 1 = 16$;

To make the number 17: $5 + 5 + 5 + 2 = 17$;

To make the number 18: $5 + 5 + 5 + 2 + 1 = 18$;

To make the number 19: $5 + 5 + 5 + 2 + 2 = 19$;

To make the number 20: $5 + 5 + 5 + 5 = 20$.

Note: Some of students' equations in their solutions may differ slightly from the ones above, as there is more than one equation to correctly make several of the numbers. For example, to make the number 2, this equation would also be correct: $5 - 2 - 1 = 2$.

Next Steps

Have students solve the following problem:

What would happen if one of the numbers (1, 2, or 5) is changed?

Which number would you change?

Extended Exploration Problems

Date: _____   Name: _____

Making Numbers

Sol says he can make all of the numbers from 1 to 20 using only the digits 1, 2 and 5 to make number sentences.

Is he right?

- Think
- Talk Together
- Solve Together
- Share

Appendix

Date: _____ Name: _____

Number Line

0 1 2 3 4 5 6 7 8 9 10 11 12 13 14 15 16 17 18 19 20

Appendix 1

Name: _____

Date: _____

Ten Frames

Appendix 2

Date: _____   Name: _____

Hundred Chart

1	2	3	4	5	6	7	8	9	10
11	12	13	14	15	16	17	18	19	20
21	22	23	24	25	26	27	28	29	30
31	32	33	34	35	36	37	38	39	40
41	42	43	44	45	46	47	48	49	50
51	52	53	54	55	56	57	58	59	60
61	62	63	64	65	66	67	68	69	70
71	72	73	74	75	76	77	78	79	80
81	82	83	84	85	86	87	88	89	90
91	92	93	94	95	96	97	98	99	100

Appendix 3

Two-Dimensional Shapes Template

Appendix 4

Three-Dimensional Objects Template

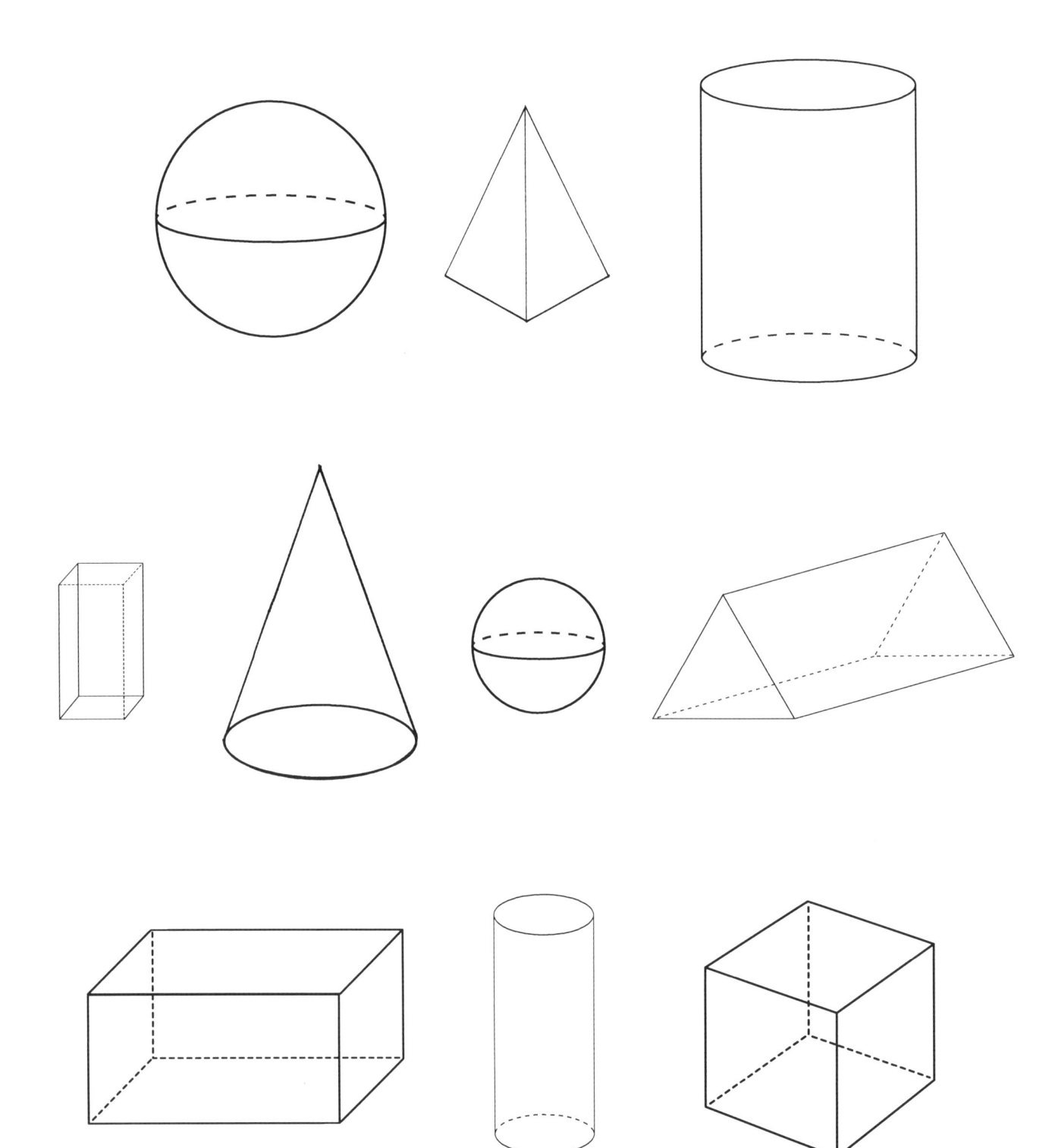

Appendix 5

References

Black, Paul et al. *Working inside the black box: Assessment for learning in the classroom.* London, UK: GL Education (formerly Granada Learning), 2004.

Brown, Peter. *The Curious Garden.* New York: Little Brown, 2009.

Cai, Jinfa and Frank Lester. "Why Is Teaching With Problem Solving Important to Student Learning? Brief." National Council of Teachers of Mathematics (NCTM) website: <http://www.nctm.org/news/content.aspx?id=25713> (accessed April 1, 2012).

Charles, Randall, Frank Lester, and Anne Bloomer. *Problem-Solving Experiences in Mathematics Grade 1,* 2nd edition. Boston: Addison-Wesley/Dale Seymour, 1994.

Davies, Anne. *Making Classroom Assessment Work*, third edition. Bloomington, IN: Solution Tree, 2011.

Government of Canada. "Eliminating the Penny." Ottawa: Department of Finance, Government of Canada, 2012 <http://www.budget.gc.ca/2012/themes/theme2-eng.html> (accessed April 1, 2012).

Hutchins, Pat. *The Doorbell Rang.* New York: Greenwillow Books, 1986.

Lawson, Jennifer. *Hands-On English Language Learning: Early Years.* Winnipeg: Portage & Main Press, 2009.

_____. *Hands-On Mathematics: Grade One.* Winnipeg: Portage & Main Press, 2007.

_____. *Hands-On Social Studies: Grade One.* Winnipeg: Portage & Main Press, 2003.

_____. *Hands-On Science: Level One.* Winnipeg: Portage & Main Press, 1999.

Rosenberg, Mary. *Daily Warm-Ups: Problem Solving Math Grade 1.* Westminster, CA: Teacher Created Resources, 2011.

Rusczyk, Richard. "What is Problem Solving?" Art of Problem Solving. <www.artofproblemsolving.com/Resources/articles.php?page=problemsolving> (accessed April 1, 2012).

Small, Marian. *Making Math Meaningful to Canadian Students, K-8.* Toronto: Nelson Education, 2008.

Van de Walle, John and LouAnn Lovin. *Teaching Student-Centered Mathematics: Grades K–3.* Boston: Pearson/Allyn and Bacon, 2005.

About the Authors

Jennifer Lawson, PhD, is the originator and senior author of all the Hands-On series. Jennifer is also a facilitator for the Manitoba Rural Learning Consortium, providing professional development for teachers and principals throughout rural Manitoba, and she teaches in the Faculty of Education at the University of Manitoba in Winnipeg, Manitoba. Jennifer is a former classroom teacher, resource/special education teacher, consultant, and principal.

Lara Jensen, BEd, BA, BPHE, has been a classroom teacher, specialist teacher, ICT integrator, curriculum coordinator, and librarian for the past 18 years at K–8 schools in Canada, Germany, and Switzerland. She holds a certificate in Outdoor and Experiential Education and has worked to incorporate inquiry-based teaching and learning into every classroom. Lara has conducted teacher's workshops on such topics as mathematics, literacy, international-mindedness, and inquiry.

Tina Jagdeo, BAH, BEd, MA, is the Learning Strategies Coordinator of the Wernham West Centre for Learning at Upper Canada College in Toronto, Ontario. In this role, she teaches boys from kindergarten to grade 7 to help them understand and develop strategies for their unique learning profiles. She enjoys leading school-based workshops on best practices in literacy, mathematics, differentiation, and social, and emotional learning. Tina has co-written two workbooks, *Centred for Learning,* volumes 1 and 2, on how to create inclusive learning environments.

Meagan Mutchmor, BEd, PBCE, is the K–8 mathematics consultant for Winnipeg School Division. She provides professional learning workshops on a variety of topics including mathematics, assessment for learning, and reflective practice. Meagan has also contributed to several educational resources as an author, advisor, and consultant. As an educator for 25 years Meagan believes that successful learners are active participants in their learning. This belief guides her practice with all learners, including children and adults.

Pat Steuart, BEd, is an elementary school teacher who has taught all subjects in primary grades 1 to 4. She currently teaches a multi-age 1–3 classroom. Pat believes in an activity-based approach to teaching and providing opportunities for students to share and discuss their solutions and ideas. She has taught courses in the Faculty of Education at the University of Manitoba. She resides in Winnipeg, Manitoba.

Dianne Soltess, BA, PBDE, is a curriculum coordinator K–8 for the St. James-Assiniboia School Division in Winnipeg, Manitoba. She has practiced in the education field for more than 30 years, teaching grades 1–6 before becoming a math/science coordinator. Dianne has taught undergraduate and post-baccalaureate courses for the Faculty of Education at the University of Manitoba in Winnipeg, Manitoba. She has been involved in math and science curriculum development and document writing for Manitoba Education and has contributed to the Hands-On Math series.

Dayna Quinn-LaFleche, BEd, is the K–4 math and math intervention teacher at Rosser Elementary School in the Interlake School Division in Rosser, Manitoba. She believes that students learn best through hands-on activities or experiences, and that when they make connections from the curriculum to real life, genuine education happens. She lives in Winnipeg, Manitoba.

Denise MacRae, BHEc, EdCert, is a former primary school teacher who taught nursery to grade 3 for 29 years in the inner city of Winnipeg. She currently works as a faculty advisor for the University of Manitoba. She lives in Winnipeg, Manitoba.

▶

Susan Atcheson, BSc in Psychology, BEd, PBCE, Certificate in Special Education, is a K–5 resource teacher in the St. James-Assiniboia School Division in Winnipeg, Manitoba. As an educator for the past 26 years, Susan has worked as an early classroom teacher with children with learning disabilities, and as a tutor for adult education. Susan believes in creating learning environments for children that engage and support curiosity and imagination while developing strong academic and social skills. As a resource teacher, she considers a collaborative approach essential to educating children.